Praise for William Martin's

A Path and a Practice

"William Martin's *A Path and a Practice* offers gentle, sensible, and attainable guidance on how anyone can find contentment in our difficult, modern world." —DINTY W. MOORE, author of *The Accidental Buddhist*

On these pages, you'll find Lao-tzu's lyrical tributes to living in the present moment, seeing the polarities of life in a positive way, accepting the Divine Feminine in all things, savoring one's experience and letting go, walking the path of gentleness and flexibility, sitting still in silence, being hospitable to all, practicing simplicity, moving beyond praise and blame, and watching things with 'the detached interest of a newborn.' The author has done a fine job giving us a vivid sense of the profundity of this spiritual classic and its relevance to our lives."
—*Spirituality and Health* magazine

Praise for William Martin's

Previous Books

"This book is pure gold. It comes as close to teaching the unteachable as anything I have ever read. If you are a parent, you have no choice—you must keep this book within reach at all times." —HUGH PRATHER, parent, minister, author of *The Little Book of Letting Go*, on *The Parent's Tao Te Ching*

"William Martin has re-rendered (*not* re-translated) Lao-tzu's ageless volume from the parental viewpoint, and lets the elegant result speak for itself."
—*Yoga Journal*, on *The Parent's Tao Te Ching*

"It's a rare thing when someone is able to improve on a classic—not only improve it but wrap it in ribbons and offer it as a gift to the modern world. It requires a man of rare wisdom, insight, and heart. Bill Martin is such a man and *The Parent's Tao Te Ching* is such a book. Not since *The Tao of Pooh* has Taoist wisdom transmogrified into something so practical, gentle, and good."
—DAN MILLMAN, author of *Way of the Peaceful Warrior*

A Path
and a
Practice

The Art of Pastoring

The Way of the Word

The Parent's Tao Te Ching

The Couple's Tao Te Ching

The Sage's Tao Te Ching

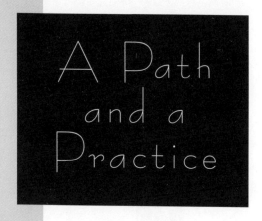

A Path and a Practice

Using Lao-tzu's
Tao Te Ching
as a Guide to an
Awakened
Spiritual Life

William Martin

With a new translation of the Tao

MARLOWE & COMPANY
NEW YORK

A PATH AND A PRACTICE: *Using Lao-tzu's Tao Te Ching*
as a Guide to an Awakened Spiritual Life
Copyright © 2005 by William Martin

Published by
Marlowe & Company
An Imprint of Avalon Publishing Group Incorporated
245 West 17th Street • 11th Floor
New York, NY 10011-5300

AVALON
publishing group incorporated

Library of Congress Cataloging-in-Publication Data
Martin, William.
A path and a practice : using Lao Tzu's Tao te ching as a guide to an awakened spiritual life /
William Martin.–1st ed.
p.cm.
ISBN 1-56924-390-5 (pbk.)
1. Laozi. Dao de jing. English. I. Title: Using Lao Tzu's Tao te ching as a guide to an awakened spiritual life. II. Laozi. Dao de jing. English. III. Title
BL1900.L35M365 2005
299.5'1482–dc22
2004022516

9 8 7 6 5 4 3

Designed by Maria Elias
Printed in Canada

To my teacher, Cheri Huber, with deepest gratitude

A Path
and a
Practice

Contents

Acknowledgments

I am filled with gratitude for the countless expressions of life that I have been privileged to meet. My deepest thanks to:

Nancy, my dear spouse and soul mate, for her love and acceptance;

the community of fellow pilgrims at the Still Point Center in Chico, California, for their fellowship and support;

my agent, Ted Weinstein, for his encouragement to write what I love; my editor and publisher, Matthew Lore, who creates beautiful books;

and finally, Lao-tzu, who 2,600 years ago gave us an expression of a path and a practice that has benefited countless beings in all lands through all the ages.

Introduction

*I*t is my great pleasure to welcome you to the path and the practice contained within the *Tao Te Ching*. This classic of Chinese wisdom literature, written almost 2,600 years ago, is one of the most loved and widely translated books in human history. Its author is traditionally considered to be Lao-tzu, a Chinese sage who lived during the fifth century BCE. Scholars enjoy debating whether or not Lao-tzu actually authored the *Tao Te Ching*. Some contend that it is a compilation of the wisdom of several authors. I am not particularly concerned with this issue for the purposes of this book. Whoever the author or authors were, they have my everlasting gratitude. I will use the name Lao-tzu—which literally means "the wise youngster"—to symbolize this gratitude.

For me, Lao-tzu's book has been much more than a beautiful collection of Chinese wisdom poetry. I have found it to be a "Tao"—a "path"—that has opened for me the experience of life in all of its beauty and all of its pain. It has been a path for me into the territory of awareness, awakening, and living in the present moment. It has also presented me with a "practice"—a way of living in freedom and joy. It has gently guided me to see how my conditioned mental habits restrict me, distract me, and cause me unnecessary suffering. For both his path and his practice I offer Lao-tzu, whoever he was, my deepest thanks.

It is this spirit of gratitude that has led me to offer my own translation of Lao-tzu. For many years I resisted this project because there are so many fine translations already in print. Why add another? But for all of their beauty and value, no modern translation has yet captured the essential thrust of the Tao as an actual path and practice—as a guide to an awakened life along with practical methods for living this life. It is this path and this practice that have blessed me with freedom and joy. It is this path and this practice that I am presenting in this book.

To aid you in extracting the elements of this path from Lao-tzu's poetic, paradoxical, and somewhat evasive style, I have included two sections in this book that I hope will be helpful. One section, entitled "The Path," is an overview that lays out the principal elements of this path in a thematic manner. This overview will give you a sense of the themes that Lao-tzu consistently weaves into his poetry, returning to them again and again, each time from a slightly different angle.

The other section I have titled "The Practice." It is located at the back of the book and will help you explore each of Lao-tzu's themes in depth. I resisted calling this section a "study guide," even though many books use that term for such sections. Studying is not the primary approach I would like you to take. As Lao-tzu might say, "Studying a thing is not experiencing a thing." You hold in your hands words that represent a living practice. Don't study it. Explore it! Walk it! Practice it!

You are not alone. This path has been walked by countless others throughout history, and is being walked by countless fellow pilgrims at the present moment. Everyone seeking a way of awakening, truth, and awareness of the present moment is your companion on this path, whatever religious or nonreligious label they might currently wear.

I would be pleased to provide whatever companionship I can. You can reach me through our center's Web site at www.thestillpoint.com. At this site, you will find the means to contact me and to participate in programs and classes that will help you in your practice. I maintain a training relationship through e-mail and phone calls with a limited number of students and it would be my delight to explore this possibility with you as well.

All my love and support I offer you.
Gassho (a bow of love),
Bill Martin
Chico, California
April 2004

1. The Path

*T*he only step necessary on your personal journey of awakening is the one that is before you at this moment. In fact, this is the only step possible for you. All of the other steps along the way are theoretical and will not be real until they, too, lie directly in your path. I am walking along on the same journey and I offer you my companionship for as long as it is helpful to you. I also offer you this introduction to and translation of Lao-tzu's wonderful text, the *Tao Te Ching*. Through his writings, this ancient sage has become my dear companion and trusted guide. It would be my pleasure if the three of us could walk along together on this path for a bit. This book will supply a format in which we can do just that. Are you ready to take the next step?

The first thing to notice is that the *Tao Te Ching* is not a linear text. It does not set out its basic premises at the beginning and then build and expand upon them in a logical progression. Each chapter is a small piece of poetry that looks at a slice of life from the perspective of Lao-tzu's path. This can be frustrating for those of us who are conditioned to assume that, in order to be helpful, books must be laid out in an orderly fashion.

Yet life is not orderly. We perceive that life unfolds in a linear fashion because our brain processes it one moment after another. But life itself is actually an infinitely complex dance in which we participate, but of which we catch only limited glimpses. Therefore the path of awareness and awakening is filled with twists, turns, backtracking, rest stops, and steep grades, all appearing in no particular order. Just when we think we can't climb another step, the trail opens into a restful meadow. Just as we are enjoying walking along a babbling brook, a canyon opens up and the trail plunges into shadow and danger. It is an ever-changing path, and each moment of travel upon it is new. Lao-tzu's book about this path has many of these same characteristics.

This ancient path has been traveled by countless pilgrims over the millennia. They have come from all lands, carrying with them a wonderful diversity of cultural and religious expressions. They have called themselves Taoists, Buddhists, Christians, Jews, Sufis, atheists, and many other names. They have established this path with compassion and mindfulness. Their courage has preserved for us a path that is open to all beings without exception. All of their sorrows and all of their joys have become part of the landscape along this path. As you walk along, one step at a time, you will be walking in their footsteps.

The only quality you need is a tiny bit of willingness. The only action you need to take is to lift your foot and take the next step.

It Is a Path of Direct Experience

**Talking about a path
is not walking that path.
Thinking about life
is not living.
[from chapter 1]**

Lao-tzu was neither a priest nor a follower of any religious belief system. He was a patient observer of the flow of life. He watched the wind move the clouds across the sky and the rain soak the earth. He watched rivers flow through wide valleys and tumble down mountain canyons. He watched the crane stand patiently by the lakeside, waiting on one leg until the water cleared to reveal a fish. He considered the contentment of the turtle sitting in the mud. He observed crops flourish one year and fail the next. He watched the seasons come and go. He saw the wonder of all things rising and falling, coming and going, living and dying. He came to understand that this wonder cannot be captured by words and concepts. It can be talked about, yet never captured. It can be thought about, yet never fathomed. It can only be experienced.

The legends that surround the formation of the *Tao Te Ching* illustrate Lao-tzu's reluctance to put his teachings into written words. One such legend speaks of a time when he became so fed up with the politics of repression in the China of his day that he got on his ox and left the country. But the border guard would not let him leave until he wrote down his wisdom for all to share. Lao-tzu said, "If I write it down it will no longer be the Tao." Nevertheless, the guard would not let him leave until he wrote something. So Lao-tzu dismounted his ox, sat in the shade of a tree, and in one afternoon wrote the short text of poetic wisdom you now have in your hands.

Legend? Undoubtedly, but a legend that speaks to the very nature of this path. It is a path of direct experience, not of abstract philosophy. It is a way of looking with clarity at the processes of life as they are, not as we think they should be. It is a path that must be walked moment by moment, and not discussed in endless words.

Yet using thoughts and words to make sense of our experience is what we humans do. It is part of our nature. Lao-tzu uses words in short poetic stanzas so that they may serve as guides and gateways to direct experience rather than as mere abstractions and distractions. This sometimes frustrates our Western conditioning, which has come to expect things to be explained without ambiguity or paradox. Such an approach forces us again and again to return to our own experience of life rather than rely on the words and teachings of others.

Directly experiencing life is not something we do easily. By the time we are adults, our experience is mediated through a multitude of conceptual filters that provide a constant commentary *about* our life, but that ignore the thing itself. This process is so deeply conditioned in most of us that we don't even notice it. We wander through day after day with our minds spinning an endless stream of thoughts, judgments, hopes, fantasies, critiques, and plans, all mixed with a babble of advertising jingles and fragments of television shows.

Lao-tzu suggests that this habitual commentary on life, though a natural part of being human, is not the same thing as a fully lived life. At the same time, he does not totally discount the conceptual thinking process. We make a certain kind of sense out of our life through the use of categories, thoughts, and words. But, as he suggests in chapter 1, these thoughts and words are gateways to life, not life itself.

How is it for you? Does the commentary in your head serve as a gateway to the deeper mystery of life? Or are you, like most of us, deeply caught in the never-ending round of judgment, effort, worry, striving, comparing, desiring, hoping, dreaming, and all the other distractions that keep you from the actual, sometimes frightening, intensity of a direct experience of life?

It Is a Path of the Present Moment

The present moment is all we have,
so we are not constantly seeking
a faster way to do things
or a better place to be.
[from chapter 80]

Every step along this path is taken in the present moment. The discrete processing nature of our brain creates the illusion that we are going somewhere and becoming someone, while in fact we are actually just experiencing a flowing stream of "present moments." There is no place to go, except here. There is no one to be, except who you are right now. This living in the present moment is an essential feature of this path.

It is also the most difficult feature to practice. As soon as we actually turn to the present moment, a thought arises that directs our attention toward some future event or to something we should have done in the past. It is almost as if the present moment is actually too frightening to really experience. An internal voice suggests that we are in too much physical or emotional pain. It hints that we really don't have the capacity to directly face this moment. It then presents an alternative from among the countless cultural diversions and distractions available.

We may also notice a voice that tells us, "If you live in the present moment, you will stop all forward progress. You will cease improving yourself and just drift through life." This voice is full of "helpful" suggestions for self-improvement. "Some later day," it suggests, "you will have things arranged well enough so that the present moment will be acceptable. Until then you'd better keep on striving."

Other voices may suggest that the present moment is impractical, unrealistic, naive, selfish, lazy, dangerous, or impossible. They may present the usual habitual daydreams, fantasies, and mental babble in order to keep us distracted and unconscious. In any case we can get a sense of how difficult such a simple-sounding thing as "living in the present moment" can actually be. Lao-tzu noticed this same difficulty and gently offered other themes throughout his book to support and encourage this practice.

It Is a Path of Opposites

**Yin and yang together
produce the energy of creation
and give rise to all things.
[from chapter 42]**

Lao-tzu's path does not lead to the elimination of the uncomfortable or the painful, or the things and qualities we have learned to call "negative." It would be more popular if it promised to lead in that direction. Instead it promises that we will learn to see the polarities of life in an entirely different way. It affirms that every polarity is absolutely necessary to the fabric of existence. The mysterious world of quantum physics reveals this basic truth. The electron with its "negative" charge and the proton with its "positive" charge exist within the atom in perfect balance. Without this basic "yin and yang" of atomic structure, nothing would exist.

Since we experience life within this physical cosmos, our basic perception of existence is that of polarities: here and there, us and them, up and down, love and fear, joy and sorrow, life and death. We naturally learn to prefer those things we call "positive"; therefore, much of our life is spent trying to experience them in isolation from their "negative" complements. This is an impossible task and only increases our fear and frustration. No matter how hard we try to make it otherwise, rising always gives way to falling; having always gives way to losing; and life always gives way to death.

This path expands our vision and leads us to a vantage point where we see all rising and falling as contained within a greater expansiveness. Life gives way to death, but death turns and gives way to life. We do not waste energy pretending otherwise, but instead trust the process of balance and return. We stop working to change the processes of life and begin to work in cooperation with them. The negative becomes the doorway to the positive. The positive is enjoyed without clinging because we know ourselves to be capable of experiencing the whole of life rather than just the parts we prefer. Our experience is no longer limited by a dependence on circumstances. Freedom becomes a permanent quality of life available anywhere, anytime.

Accepting what is, we find it to be perfect.
[from chapter 22]

Acceptance is courageous attention turned to the nature of things as they truly are, not as we wish them to be. This attention enables our natural wisdom and energy to work effectively with circumstances. It allows us to avoid the twin traps of either hiding our heads in the sand while events roll over us or wearing ourselves out, making things worse by frenetic and ineffective activity. Acceptance allows us to fully understand events and circumstances, freeing us to participate in life with joy and abandon. We become as patient as a still pond, yet as potentially powerful as a rushing river.

Our conditioning will insist that, if we accept life as it is, it will never change. We will become the passive victims of fate. Evil and suffering will roll on unopposed. In fact, Lao-tzu insists, just the opposite is true. Without a deep and courageous acceptance of the "is-ness" of life, our actions become distorted by our need to impose our opinions, ideas, and solutions on life without understanding the true nature of things. We end by standing outside of situations and attempting to "fix" them from this illusory vantage point. This approach has never worked and it never will.

I spent many years as a counselor in private practice. During that time I worked with many people who lived in abusive situations. None of my well-meaning attempts to "fix" these situations ever worked. One day a woman was sitting in my office in silence for many minutes as I gave up trying to find the right words. She stared at the carpet for a long time and then she looked up. "He abuses me," she said. "He abuses me," she repeated, "and nothing I've tried to do has ever changed that." She sat up straight and shouted, "He abuses me!" From that moment her life began to change. Her acceptance of the reality of her situation set her free to take action. Nonacceptance keeps patterns intact. Acceptance sets us free.

It Is a Universal Path

There are no "special favorites" along this path.
It unfolds itself before whoever walks along it.
[from chapter 79]

This path is our true home
because it is home to all things
in heaven and on earth.
[from chapter 25]

Lao-tzu's approach is distrustful of formal religions and does not talk about belief systems. He does not advocate the esoteric form of Taoist religion that was prevalent in the China of his time—a Taoism of magic, monasteries, rituals, and beliefs. His path stands outside such practices and asks nothing from those who follow it except that they pay attention. It does not present rules or doctrines to which one must assent. It presents only observations of the way the Tao seems to work in everyday life and encouragement to follow the same pattern in our lives.

This path, then, is available to persons of any religious system or of no religious system. It does not require that we give up rituals; nor does it require that we adopt any. Rituals and systems can play a helpful role within this practice, or they can be completely absent. Christians, Buddhists, Muslims, and atheists are all equally welcome. There are no "people of the Tao" who are set apart from any other people. Everything and everyone in the cosmos is an expression of the Tao. Everyone emerges from the Tao and everyone is ever contained within the Tao.

The only distinction Lao-tzu would make is the observation that those who practice mindful attention to the process of the Tao will experience the contentment, freedom, and joy that come from understanding oneself to be a part of life in all its mystery and wonder. It is as if someone within us draws a huge, even infinite, circle that takes in everything that is and then says, "To this I belong!"

It Is the Path of Our True Nature

**Free of conditioned thinking,
we experience our true nature.
Caught in conditioned thinking,
we experience only who we think we are.
[from chapter 1]**

In this translation I use phrases such as "conditioned thinking" and "conditioned nature" to refer to that part of our self-identity that arises from our natural need to find safety and belonging within our families, communities, societies, and world. Our brain naturally processes information in a discrete manner, separating an almost infinite array of sensory input into separate categories of "this" and "that." After a few years of this process we develop a sense of "self" as one more "this" as opposed to, or separate from, all the other "thats." Of course we become concerned with the protection of and the well-being of this separate "self" and thus create a life of fear, tension, resistance, and suffering.

There is nothing wrong with this process of conditioning. It is part of life. The problem, says Lao-tzu, arises when we mistake this conditioning for our true nature; when we believe that this is who we really are rather than just one limited way of seeing ourselves. The path of Lao-tzu accepts this conditioning as a necessary stage of development, but a stage that must be transcended in order to experience the full freedom life has to offer. So our practice along this path helps us see through our conditioning to discover our true nature.

Lao-tzu uses the character "p'u," which literally means "uncarved block," to indicate that part of our nature that is not conditioned, that is our original nature. I have sometimes translated this as "true nature" to indicate that it stands outside our ego structures and needs. It stands apart from all of our conditioned fears. Within our true nature, change, loss, pain, separation, and death all take their turns as our life unfolds, but are not overlaid with a blanket of anxiety and resistance.

This true nature does not need improvement. This is why I so often insist that this path is not a path of self-improvement. The conditioned mind derives great benefit from self-improvement programs because they insure that there will always be a "self" to improve. Yet paradoxically, as we touch our true nature, the peace and satisfaction that self-improvement programs promise begin to appear; however, this peace and satisfaction are no longer dependent on the fragile foundation of effort. They now arise from the assurance of "the way things really are." So as we walk along this path we become gradually more acquainted with the truth of our existence. We are not forming ourselves into some spiritual ideal. We are experiencing what we already are.

It Is a Path of Letting Go

**This is a path of letting go
so there will be room to live.
[from chapter 9]**

Thinking ourselves somehow separate from life, we conclude that our safety and well-being are dependent on our ability to control our circumstances. Attempting to control circumstances, we separate ourselves from those circumstances to such a degree that we end up bringing to ourselves and to others misery rather than the promised safety. Lao-tzu teaches us to let go. We let go of the belief that control is possible. We let go of the notion that our efforts at control will keep us safe. We let go of the countless conditioned beliefs that have promised safety and happiness, only to deliver anxiety and suffering. We eventually let go even of the ideas of who we are as a separate ego.

This path accepts that developing an ego is an essential element in human growth. But it also suggests that this development might be a *stage* of human development rather than its end product. Developing a cocoon is a natural and essential part of being a caterpillar. But the time comes when the cocoon softens, wears out, and opens up. What if this is the case for all of our opinions, possessions, and even for our ego? What if, when the cocoon of ego opens, instead of the feared abyss we find a butterfly?

It Is a Path of Flexibility

This is the secret of our path:
gentleness and flexibility
bring the results
that force and rigidity
fail to achieve.
[from chapter 36]

Lao-tzu often uses water as a symbol for the power of flexibility. All water on earth has its origin in the ocean. From the ocean it rises to the clouds, drifts across the sky, and begins its return to the ocean. Sometimes it falls directly back to the ocean. Sometimes it falls on land and makes its way back to the ocean through streams, lakes, and rivers. Whatever water meets along the way, it embraces. Yet nothing stops it from returning. It does not ask if it is taking the "right" path to its home. It knows that all paths are paths of return. It is patient, powerful, and irresistible in its acceptance of its path. Obstacles are never a problem. It will flow around, cascade over, seep under, wear away, or evaporate and fall on the other side of any obstacle.

Notice how our conditioned voices will characterize flexibility as wishy-washy, indecisive, weak, and ineffective. These learned mental habits insist that the goal of life is to resist, fight, and defeat the people and events that are labeled "obstacles" to whatever the same mental habits have decreed we must accomplish in order to be a "success" at life.

On this path, however, success is assured. Like water, we are on a journey home. And, like water, we will accomplish that journey in spite of any seeming obstacle presented by people, events, or especially, by our own thoughts and fears. As we learn to trust this truth, we begin to naturally have the patience and flexibility of water. Encountering a seeming obstacle or frustration, we remember that the ultimate success of our journey is assured; therefore, we relax and allow ourselves to fully experience and comprehend our current situation. As we allow this full experience and comprehension to emerge, we naturally flow into the most effective next step. The rigidity of our conditioned ideas about who we are and what we have to do in certain situations dissolves, and we find that we have the natural flexibility to accomplish whatever is necessary.

IT IS AN EFFORTLESS PATH

This is why we practice
"effortless effort."
We act without ado.
We teach without arguments.
[from chapter 43]

Lao-tzu makes extensive use of the character combination *wu-wei*, which literally means "not-doing doing." This phrase implies pure action in the present moment without any accompanying resistance, second-guessing, or worry. In the practice of wu-wei we just "do what we do." The more awareness and acceptance we bring to the present moment, the more wu-wei is possible. This can take the form of either energetic activity or relaxed waiting.

Like acceptance, wu-wei is not passive, though it may sometimes seem that way when its wisdom indicates relaxed waiting in the midst of our countless cultural messages of "hurry, hurry, hurry, do something!" The paradox of wu-wei is seen when, at a time when our conditioned thoughts are trying to distract or immobilize us, we find a flow of energy arising that keeps us working at a task with a focus and an ease we never expected.

Wu-wei is closely tied to awareness of the present moment. With this awareness we clearly see what action is appropriate. Not being constantly drawn off into past or future fantasies, we intuitively know what to do. Our actions become expansive and creative. We are able to understand and take into account a multitude of factors without being immobilized. Thoughts arise and pass away without distracting us from the task at hand.

It Is a Meditative Path

**Sitting still allows us to notice
the subtle stirrings of the mind.
[from chapter 64]**

Lao-tzu consistently calls us back to a meditative stillness that creates a space in which we can experience the wonders of our life. This meditative stillness includes both formal times of meditative practice and the internal stillness that is our refuge in the midst of a hurried day.

Taoist meditation is a simple practice. It requires no special equipment, atmosphere, or preparation. It can be helpful to have a comfortable cushion to sit on, but it is not necessary. Many people enjoy meditating while standing up. It can be helpful to meditate in restful surroundings, but it is not necessary. The purpose of meditative practice is to cultivate the ability to be present in a restful yet alert state wherever we are. It can be helpful to learn various techniques, but it is not necessary. The great Taoist and Zen masters used the simple inhalation and exhalation of the breath as their focus.

We do not meditate to create altered states of consciousness. In fact, most of modern life is spent in altered states of consciousness and meditation is the practice of returning to an *unaltered* state. Therefore we simply sit or stand quietly and pay attention to the way the breath enters and leaves the body. We allow our mind to go down whatever rabbit trails it will. We just gently return our attention to our breath and stop following our mind down those trails.

We do not meditate to still the mind, though a certain kind of stillness can accompany meditation. We meditate to watch and to understand the mind. We gradually begin to see the ways in which it has been conditioned to resist, distract, fantasize, worry, plan, and in general keep us from actually living our lives. As we see this activity, we are able to compassionately return again and again to the present moment by simply noticing the breath.

We do not meditate to bring ourselves peace, though a deep peace is part of our true nature. On the surface, many meditation periods are filled with turmoil, pain, and frustration. Our mind has been creating this turmoil for decades and stopping to pay attention to it is, especially at first, not at all fun. Often what we assume was a "bad" meditation was actually doing exactly what meditation is designed to do—show us how we have learned to resist our life.

The third section of this book, "The Practice," contains many suggestions for the uses of meditation. There is no right way to meditate and there is no "bad" meditation. We are simply committing ourselves to paying attention to our life. We use meditation to help us in that attention process. We are not trying to become good meditators. We are trying to wake up.

It Is a Path of the Next Step

**It is the single small step
that begins the journey of a thousand miles.
[from chapter 64]**

No matter how vast the chasm between where we are and where we sense we are headed appears, the only action we can ever take is right here, right now—a simple step. No matter how complicated the consequences of that step seem to be, we will never really know until we take the step, and then the next one, and the next one.

The *Tao Te Ching* is an invitation from Lao-tzu to take that next step. These are the last words I am writing in the formal draft of this book. I trust my editor to make helpful changes that will create a more helpful book, but at this point in time I am done. I will turn off my computer now and turn to the next small step, a birthday dinner with my dear wife. Perhaps turning the page and entering the second section of this book, "The Tao," will be your next step. Perhaps you will close the book and go out to dinner yourself. We just keep stepping along on our thousand-mile journey. Enjoy it.

2 ▪ The Tao

1 ▪ Direct Experience

Talking about a path
is not walking that path.
Thinking about life
is not living.

Directly experiencing life
brings unconditional appreciation
and unity.
Thinking about life
brings conditional judgments
and separation.

Free of conditioned thinking,
we experience our true nature.
Caught in conditioned thinking,
we experience only who we think we are.

Yet both our conditioned nature
and our true nature
are part of life itself.
Our conditioned experience of living
is a gateway to unconditional life.

Beauty cannot exist
without ugliness.
Virtue cannot exist
without vice.
Living, we know death.
Struggling, we know ease.
Rising high, we know the depths.
Being quiet, we understand noise.

Everything gives rise to its opposite,
therefore we work without conscious effort,
and teach without agenda.
We enjoy everything
and possess nothing.
Our accomplishments
do not emerge from our ego,
so we do not cling to them.
Thus they benefit all beings.

If achievement is valued,
jealousy will result.
If possessions are valued,
hoarding and stealing will result.

Therefore this path is one
of contentment and simplicity.
It empties the mind of its chattering,
and fills the soul with truth.
It frees us from our wanting
and returns us to our passion.

No longer needing to have our own way,
we are not fooled by clever plots and plans.
Our actions become focused, pure, and effortless.

4 ▪ The Bounty of Life

Walking this path,
we experience inexhaustible energy.
From what appears an empty void,
we find the bounty of life.

Our edginess, tension,
anger, and turmoil
begin to settle down.
In their place we find
a deep tranquility
that has been here waiting
since before the beginning
of beginning-less time.

Life has no preferences.
Every manifestation has its place
and lives its life under the sun.
Therefore we welcome
everything and everyone
without distinction.

Life continuously breathes
its forms into existence,
never depleting itself,
always replenishing itself.

Clinging to our preferences,
we separate ourselves from life
and suffer exhaustion.
Sitting still and following our breath,
we find renewal.

6 ▪ The Mother of All

Everything that exists was born
of the feminine principle within the Tao.
This mysterious principle can be called
"the mother of all."

There is no need
to weary ourselves in an effort to find her.
She is ever with us
because she *is* us.

7 ▪ The Watcher

How can we find the eternal,
the lasting nature of the Tao,
that seems so elusive amid the changes of life?

The Tao does not come and go
as do all formations.
It is the watcher of the comings
and the goings.

In our practice we find
that we are the watcher as well.
We watch our opinions and ideas,
our likes and dislikes,
our desires and our fears,
our bodies and our minds,
but we do not identify with them.
Therefore, when they arise,
we watch.
When they pass away,
we remain.

8 ▪ Our Life Flows like Water

Our true nature is like water.
It doesn't decide whom to nurture
and whom to avoid.
It doesn't decide that some tasks
are too distasteful.
It just flows like a river to the ocean,
nurturing everything in its path.
This is the nature of the Tao within all people.

Living by this principle,
we choose dwellings that are simple and humble.
We meditate to cultivate quiet
and serene thoughts.
We treat all beings with loving-kindness.
We speak with compassion and clarity.
We manage our lives for the benefit of all beings.
We live in awareness of the present moment
and take action only when the time is right.

In this manner, our life flows like water
and fulfills itself naturally.

9 ▪ A Path of Letting Go

This is a path of letting go
so there will be room to live.

If we hold on to opinions,
our minds will become dull and useless.
Let go of opinions.

If we hold on to possessions,
we will always be at risk.
Let go of possessions.

If we hold on to ego,
we will continue to suffer.
Let go of ego.

Working without thought of praise or blame
is the way of true contentment.

Can we embrace both the acceptable
and unacceptable parts of ourselves?
Can we breathe as easily as innocent babies?
Can we see the world clearly
and without judgment?
Can we act with loving-kindness
yet remain unknown and unsung?
Can we watch all things come and go,
yet remain undisturbed?
Can we accept our countless thoughts and opinions,
yet not take them seriously?

If we can do this we are acting
according to the virtue that is naturally ours;
nourishing all things, but possessing nothing;
enjoying all things, but clinging to nothing;
working diligently,
but claiming credit for nothing;
growing in wisdom, but controlling nothing.

The spokes and the hub
are the visible parts of a wheel.
The wheel is useful because it spins about
the invisible point at its center.

Clay is the material from which a pot is made.
The pot is useful because of the empty space inside the form.

A house is made with walls, doors, and windows.
The house becomes a home for people
through the quality of life lived within.

We practice with the visible and tangible,
but it is the invisible and intangible within us
that bring us life.

Trying to see everything,
we become blind.
Listening to every voice,
we become confused.
Attempting to satisfy all our appetites
we become weary.
Being driven this way and that
by our conditioning
makes us crazy.
Buying more things
only wastes our energy.

Outer things exist,
but do not define us.
We are mysterious and internal
not obvious and external.

13 ▪ All Things as Ourselves

Expecting either praise or blame
makes us anxious.
Seeing ourselves as separate and isolated
makes us suffer.

What are the implications of
"expecting either praise or blame
makes us anxious"?
To desire praise is to fear blame.
To fear blame is to desire praise.
Both are rooted in fear
and bound up in desire.
That is why on this path
there is neither praise nor blame.

What are the implications of
"seeing ourselves as separate and isolated
makes us suffer"?
We are all expressions of the one life
of the Tao.
Seeing ourselves as separate is a mistake
that leaves us feeling vulnerable.
We use countless strategies

to protect ourselves from this vulnerable feeling.
This is the root of our suffering.

Knowing that we are part of everything that is,
we care for and nurture all things as ourselves.

What we are seeking
can't be seen, heard, or touched.
It is our essential unity
beyond the divisions of our senses.

It is not obvious to the mind,
but neither is it hidden from the heart.

Looking at nothing,
all of a sudden there it is!
But the moment we see it, it disappears,
leaving only a vague memory.

Chasing after it is useless
because it didn't begin anytime
and isn't going anywhere.
To realize our true nature,
we need only return to our breath,
here and now.

The freedom of enlightenment
is impossible to describe.
We can only notice how it appears in action.

We pay complete attention
to whatever we are doing,
as if we were crossing a river
on ice-covered stones.
We are alert to everything that happens,
like a bird watching in all directions.
We have a quiet dignity and reserve,
like a guest who does not seek attention.
Our judgments and opinions have melted away,
like ice in the summer heat.
There is a beautiful simplicity about us,
like a gem before it is shaped and polished.
We welcome whatever comes,
as a valley welcomes the river.

To notice this enlightenment,
we sit patiently and wait
for muddy thoughts to settle
and our mind to become clear.
Life then lives itself in us.

Practicing this path, we no longer worry
about what we have or don't have
because we have everything!

When the chatter of our mind quiets down,
we find the still point
around which all of life revolves.
From this still point we watch everything
come and go in perfect peace.

Everything that is, was, or ever will be
has a common source from which it comes,
in which it lives,
and to which it returns.

Understanding this coming and going,
we return to our source and our confusion ends.
Not understanding this, we remain confused
and bring about great suffering.

Living at the still point, we are open to all of life.
Open to all of life, we don't judge anything.
Not judging, we see with compassion.
Seeing with compassion,
we discover our true nature.
Discovering our true nature,
we are at home
and nothing in life disturbs us.

The deepest virtue is to be unaware
of a separate self at all.
Being aware of a separate self,
it is good to have compassion for that self.
Not having compassion for our self,
we become afraid of our own nature.
Being afraid of our own nature,
we come to actually hate our self.
Hating our self,
how can we value anyone else?

Free from self-hate,
our actions are not burdened
by our need for attention.
Therefore people say,
"It happened naturally."

18 ▪ A Pretense of Life

When we forget who we truly are,
we turn to external rules
to define goodness and morality.
When we no longer live from our heart,
we search for clever strategies
to guide our actions.
This is only a pretense of life.

Duty and loyalty become substitutes
for our inability to love ourselves
and others.
Then we insist our leaders heal the suffering
created by our own divided minds.

If we give up our attempts to be holy and wise,
everyone, including ourselves,
will greatly benefit.
If we give up our rules for goodness and justice,
all beings will naturally be treated
with loving-kindness.
If we give up striving to accumulate by clever means,
theft will disappear.

But these lessons are mere outward forms.
The core of our path is this:
we see through our conditioned mind
and find our true nature waiting.

We always strive to make the right choice,
and always fear the wrong choice.
We pursue what others say is good,
and avoid what others say is bad.
How sad this is for us!
People are constantly stirred up
like children at a circus—
always looking for the next act to entertain them.
But this practice asks us to remain undisturbed,
and watch all things
with the detached interest of a newborn.

In a culture where excess accumulation is the norm,
this path seems idiotic.
Fearful voices in our mind warn us
that we will end up wandering the street,
homeless and alone.
We are urged to be clever and successful
and always in control.
But this practice asks us to relinquish the illusion of control
and to be content with whatever comes our way.

This seems so strange
and different from the usual way.
But it is the way of life itself.

This path brings us to our true nature.

Though this way seems elusive
and avoids our words and concepts,
it is the source of everything
seen and unseen.

Though walking this path
seems to take us into deep
and hidden shadows,
it leads us into the very
life force of all things.
Since before the beginning
of beginning-less time,
it has been both creator of,
and witness to, all existence.

We know the truth of this way,
not by believing it,
but by being it.

Accepting what is, we find it to be perfect.
What seemed distorted is seen as true.
What seemed lacking is seen as abundant.
What seemed worn out is seen as fresh and new.

Possessing little, we are content.
Too much stuff and we lose our way.

When we reside at the center,
our actions nurture all things.
We don't act out of ego needs,
so our actions are enlightened.
We don't claim to be perfect,
so our ideas are welcomed.
We aren't looking for reward,
so our teaching is enduring
and accessible to all.
We don't try to control or convince anyone,
so opposition is not an issue.

"Accept what is,
and find it to be perfect"
is not an idle phrase.
Acceptance of life
is the only path to wholeness.

This is a path of few words.
Silence is the natural way of life.
Strong winds arise,
and pass away.
Torrential rains arise,
and pass away.
Even the cosmos,
which produces the wind and rain,
passes away.
Why then so much concern
over what to do
and what to say?

Our life is an expression of life itself.
Our true nature expresses itself
in everything we do.
Success and failure are seen
as part of a seamless joyful whole.
Each is accepted
and fully lived.

Stretching to reach it,
we fall.
Running to catch it,
we get lost.
Pretending to be enlightened,
we become dim and foolish.
Trying to "do it right,"
we fail.
Looking for praise,
we receive nothing.
Grabbing hold of it,
we lose it.

All of this strutting, striving,
straining, and grasping
is excess baggage.
The very freedom it promises does not appear
until we lay it down.

This path we follow existed
before the universe was born.

It contains within itself
unchanging tranquility and solitude.
It is present wherever we turn
and provides inexhaustible compassion
to all beings.
Thus it may be considered
the mother of the universe.
It has no name, but if we have to refer to it
we call it Tao.

It can also be called the great mystery
from which we come, in which we live,
and to which we return.

It is a path filled with the grandeur
of the cosmos, the earth,
and the human heart.

This path is our true home
because it is home to all things
in heaven and on earth.

26 ▪ Why Scurry About?

Because this path is deeply rooted,
it allows us to be light-hearted
and not take ourselves too seriously.
Because this path is stable,
it allows us to act without rashness.

So, whatever we do,
we do not abandon ourselves.
Even though the world provides
endless worries and distractions,
we remain unconcerned and content.

We have everything we could want.
Why would we scurry about
looking for something else?
Only if we lose touch with our true nature
are we trapped in agitation and hurry.

This path has no rules, no rituals,
and no preconceived notions.
Traveling it we seek neither praise nor blame,
yet our actions become impeccable and blameless.

Our life is illumined by the light.
Everything that happens
is for our benefit.
Everything in our experience
instructs us in the way.
Everyone we meet becomes our teacher,
good and bad alike.
Everyone we meet becomes our student,
bright and dull alike.
If we try to pick and choose,
we will never learn.

Ceasing to pick and choose:
this is the great secret of life.

Striving to make our way in the world
seems prudent.
But if we trust our heart
we may find the way opening
with the effortless ease
of a budding flower.

Striving to live a life of virtue
is approved of by all.
But if we trust our heart
we may find the power of our true nature
everywhere we turn,
in everyone we meet.

Charismatic personalities
capture our attention.
But it is our true nature,
existing beneath our personality,
that brings power and purpose to our life.

Separate from our true nature,
we create forms and functions
and struggle to make them work.
Returning to our original nature,

we use the forms and functions
for the benefit of all.

Attempting to control external events
will never keep us safe.
Control is an illusion.

Whatever we try to control,
we separate from ourselves.
Whatever we try to fix,
we ruin.
Life is sacred,
and flows exactly as it should.

We return to our breathing.
It knows exactly what to do,
rising and falling without conscious control.
In the same way
we sometimes have an excess
and sometimes have a lack.
We sometimes assert ourselves,
and sometimes hold back.
We sometimes succeed,
and sometimes fail completely.

Our practice is to see all this
without taking it seriously.

That way we do not abandon ourselves.
We remain at peace.

Practicing this path,
we do not struggle.
To struggle is to invite resistance.
To invite resistance is to create suffering
in our life,
and in the world.

Paying attention to the present moment,
we see the things that we must do.
We do them without complaint, resistance,
or second-guessing,
then we stop.
We don't complicate our actions
by seeking control or recognition.

Correct action, however difficult,
is naturally focused and effective.
Adding struggle complicates
and does not lead to lasting good.

31 ▪ Weep That This Has Happened

Weapons of violence
are contrary to the common good,
no matter how skillfully used.
So we vow to do no harm.

Faced with unavoidable violence
we remember this vow,
act quickly,
and return immediately to peace.

Battles are not with "enemies"
but with beings like ourselves.
Knowing this, we do not rejoice in victory
nor take delight in the downfall of others.
Victory is an illusion and gains us nothing.

Once a battle is over we lay our weapons down
and weep that this has happened.

What we call the Tao
really has no name.
Naming something, we think we understand it.
What we call the Tao is far too subtle for that.
We experience it in our own true nature.
If we hold on to our own true nature,
all external and internal strife falls away.
Peace descends on our lives
like a gentle rain from heaven.
Joy flows from the earth
like a mighty river.
There is no need to urge ourselves
to do good.
Goodness is our heart's true nature.

The more we use words,
the more distinctions we make.
The more distinctions we make,
the more we suffer.
When we stop taking distinctions seriously,
we cease to suffer.
We return to peace
just as streams and rivers
return to the ocean.

Studying other people
brings us knowledge.
Studying our own mind
brings us freedom.
Overcoming other people
requires force.
Overcoming our conditioning
requires true power.
Once we realize that we always have
everything we need,
we understand that we are truly
adequate for our life.

Identifying with our true nature,
we also discover that we are adequate
for our death as well.

The great Tao is like an ocean.
It fills the universe
and all things rely upon it.
It gives us birth
and never abandons us.

It does all this marvelous work
and needs no recognition.
It nourishes and sustains us
yet does not claim to own us.
It has no need for glory
so it blends into the background
and is hardly ever noticed.
It is the true home to which we return,
yet it wants no worship.
No wonder we consider it great.

Our own greatness doesn't come
from power or control.
We just live our lives each moment
as the greatness that we are.

Our practice looks beneath
the passing thoughts that seem so real.
Clinging to them brings pain.
Letting them come and go
brings peace.

Lively music and good food
may capture our attention,
but speaking of this path
is not exciting.
People would rather try to make things work,
look for distractions,
and listen to empty promises.

We turn to this path
only when we have exhausted
all other paths.

36 ▪ This Is the Secret of Our Path

If we try to get rid of something,
it will naturally remain.
If we try to weaken a habit,
it will naturally remain strong.
If we try to push away our thoughts,
they will naturally return.
If we try to get rid of our pain,
we will suffer all the more.

This is the secret of our path:
gentleness and flexibility
bring the results
that force and rigidity
fail to achieve.

Our true benefit lies
not in our words or arguments,
but in the depth of our practice.

37 ▪ As If We Do Nothing

Our practice is one of
effortless effort.
It seems as if we do nothing,
yet everything is done.

If we stay on this path
and resist the temptation to control,
each thing will naturally evolve
according to its individual nature.

When our conditioning arises
and attempts to stir us up,
we return to the simple stillness
of our natural state.
When we abide at this still point
our conditioned habits naturally fall away,
leaving only peace.

Not trying to be good,
we experience natural goodness.
Being good, while hoping for reward,
has nothing to do with natural goodness.
Natural goodness works effortlessly
and benefits all.
Contrived goodness requires great effort
and accomplishes very little.
Compassion acts and seeks nothing.
Justice acts and seeks specific results.
Morality acts, then demands,
and then forces correct behavior.
When we are separated from our true nature,
we turn to rules of goodness.
When we fail at being good,
we make more detailed rules
to govern our relationships.
When our relationships suffer,
we insist on justice and fairness.
Not finding justice or fairness,
we all agree to pretend
that empty rituals will suffice.

Our practice is to see through this artificial effort
and choose to trust in our true nature.
With that choice, our suffering ends.

With this practice we find clarity.
Our horizons become expansive.
Our daily life becomes tranquil.
Our souls become inspired.
Our relationships become filled
with trust and honesty.
Our society flourishes.
Everything around us becomes
filled with creative life.

Without this practice we continue to suffer.
Our horizons contract.
Our daily life fills with anxiety.
Our souls wither.
Our relationships crumble.
Our society flounders.
Everything around us seems exhausted.

Despite our seeming prestige and power,
we know that we are really little children,
dependent on the Tao and helpless without it.

A wagon rolls along and does its job
with no fanfare at all.

Rather than clattering about
trying to be noticed,
we just roll along
like common stones in the river.

Following this path
returns us to our root.
It is a tender and gentle path.

Everything in the cosmos
depends on everything else.
Even our experience of life
depends upon our death.

The most helpful response to this path
is to devote ourselves to it
and practice it diligently.
But most people practice it only half-heartedly,
and some people disregard it entirely,
seeing it as absurd.
The Tao reflects to us our own inner attitudes.
This is its greatness.

So we can establish a set of helpful maxims:
The way to clarity will seem confusing.
The way to progress
will seem like going backwards.
The smoothest way will seem filled with obstacles.
The greatest power will lie in receptivity.
True innocence will appear shameful.
The greatest resources will appear inadequate.
Genuine goodness will appear suspect.
The truly solid and dependable
will seem uncertain.
Effective boundaries will be limitless.
The wisest person will always be learning.

The most pleasing music is hidden in silence.
The most beautiful art begins without form.
And so this path itself, silent and without form,
is the way to all beauty and joy.

Hidden in the mystery of the Tao
lies the original unity.
This unity contains the duality
of yin and yang.
Yin and yang together
produce the energy of creation
and give rise to all things.

Every atom of the cosmos
contains the yin and the yang together.
We feel this harmonious process
in the rising and falling
of our breath.

It seems natural to avoid loss and seek gain,
but on this path such distinctions are not helpful.
There is no gain without loss.
There is no fullness without deprivation.
Who knows how or when
one gives way to the other.
So we remain at the center
and trust events instead of forcing them.
This is the heart of all spiritual paths.

43 ▪ Act without Ado

The most fluid and yielding substance
will flow past the most rigid
with the speed of a racehorse.
That which does not hold a particular form
can enter even that which seems impenetrable.
This is why we practice
"effortless effort."
We act without ado.
We teach without arguments.

This is the way of true happiness,
but because people prefer distractions and noise,
it is not a popular way.

Is fame worth the sacrifice
of our true nature?
Does wealth compensate
for the loss of ourselves?
Which causes more suffering—
accumulating things,
or letting them all go?

Looking outside ourselves
for approval and security,
we find only suffering.
Understanding that we are capable for our lives,
we stop exhausting ourselves
and begin enjoying ourselves.

45 ▪ Exactly What Is Needed

True perfection does not exhaust itself
trying to appear perfect.
True abundance does not waste itself
in showy displays.

The most direct path
will appear to wind about.
The greatest skill
will appear quite ordinary.
The most helpful words
will appear hesitant.

When we see clearly,
we act with tranquility,
and exactly what is needed is done.

When we practice this path
our energy is focused on useful, helpful tasks.
When we depart from this path,
fear contaminates our energy
and we become concerned with self-protection.

Our greatest suffering comes
from not knowing who we are
or where we belong.
Our greatest unhappiness comes
from always wanting something more,
something else.

To be content with each breath
is to be eternally content.
This is our practice.

It is not necessary to travel
to understand the world.
It is not necessary to look out the window
to see into ourselves.

The more we look outside ourselves for knowledge,
the less we know about anything.

We do not wander about
yet still we gain knowledge.
We do not look about
yet still we gain understanding.
We do not strive
yet still we accomplish everything.

Seeking knowledge,
we add new facts each day.
Seeking the Tao,
we drop assumptions each day.
Each day we assume less and less
until we assume nothing.
There is nothing left to do,
and nothing left undone.

Allowing things to come and go
according to their nature,
we gain everything.
Trying to control everything,
we gain nothing.

We hold no fixed opinions.
Our hearts are therefore open
to the hearts of all.

We extend kindness to the kind
and unkind alike.
Thus kindness becomes our very nature.

We extend trust to the trustworthy
and untrustworthy alike.
Thus trust becomes our very nature.

We don't contend with people
by seeking to gain advantage.
People around us lose their edge
and we become loving friends
to the whole world.

Life and death are inseparable.
One is form and the other is formless.
Each gives way to the other.
One third of people concentrate on life
and ignore death.
One third obsess over death
and ignore life.
One third don't think of either
and just pass on through.
Each clings to conditioned ideas.
Each suffers.

Walking this path
we become skillful
at living without suffering.
We do not fear attack,
therefore an attacker
has already lost the advantage.
Life and death have become the same;
therefore even death cannot disturb us.

The Tao expresses itself
in each and every being.
Its very presence nurtures us.
We are shaped and perfected by it
in the living of our lives.
Therefore each and every being honors the Tao
and delights in its presence,
not because they are commanded,
but because it is their nature.

We are expressions of the Tao.
Its presence sustains us,
develops us,
teaches us,
shelters us,
matures us,
and returns us to our origin.

The Tao gives us life
but does not claim to own us.
It is ever acting on our behalf
but expects nothing in return.
It is our true guide
but does not control us.

Its presence is deep within
the heart of every being.

The origin of all that is
can naturally be called "mother of all."
Finding our mother, we find our true self.
Finding our true self,
our suffering ends.

If we let our thoughts become still
and our needs become few,
we will live in peace.
If we follow our thoughts
and chase after distractions,
we will live in chaos.

Noticing small and ordinary things
is enlightenment.
Treating all beings with kindness
is strength.

Enlightenment is our natural state.
Sitting in meditation we see our hidden suffering,
accept it, lay it down,
and return to peace.

53 ■ A Tiny Bit of Willingness

It takes just a tiny bit of willingness
to follow this path,
but many things distract us.
This path is broad and steady
but we are conditioned to follow our thoughts
down countless sidetracks.

Those who can afford distractions
gather them by the carload,
while the basic needs of most go unmet.
The accumulation of luxuries
is contrary to this path.
It is a futile attempt to find happiness by taking
that which is not freely given.

If we establish ourselves on this path,
we will not be shaken by events.
If we take it into our hearts,
our children and their children will benefit.

This path returns us to our true self.
It brings our families abundant joy.
It brings our communities a lasting legacy.
It brings our countries true prosperity.

All that is expresses this path.
Therefore we practice awareness
in each and every moment.
We see ourselves in every person we meet.
The whole world becomes our family,
our community,
our country.

How do we make this discovery?
By sitting still and looking within.

Embracing this path
we are like newborn children.
We are in natural harmony with all creatures,
bringing harm to none.
Our body is soft and flexible, yet strong.
Our vital passion is not limited
to sexual intercourse,
but empowers all of life.
Our harmony and focus allow us
to work all day at a single task
and not grow tired.

This harmony is experienced
only in the present moment.
It is in the present moment
that we see the way ahead.
Everything in life becomes a blessing.
Forcing events to be other than they are
only brings us misery.

The more we understand this path,
the less we need to convince others.
The more we need to convince others,
the less we really understand.

So we become silent.
We stop looking about for approval.
We cease taking offense
at the opinions of others.
We no longer complicate our thinking
or our lives.
We do not seek the spotlight
but instead become a simple part of all that is.

We can be loved or shunned,
make a profit or suffer a loss,
be honored or disgraced,
and never lose the treasure of our being.

To guide a country
we use administrative skills.
To wage a war
we use surprise tactics.
But to gain joy in living
we let life live itself.

What does "let life live itself" mean?
The harder we try
the more our efforts fail.
The more we arm ourselves
the more chaos we experience.
The more schemes we plan
the less predictable are the results.
The more rules we impose
the more we become rule-breakers.

So in this practice
we stop trying to change ourselves
and find that we naturally change.
We stop trying to be good
and find that goodness is our nature.
We stop trying to get rich,
and find that our life is full of abundance.

We stop trying to get our own way
and find that we enjoy our life.

This path is unobtrusive,
allowing the simple purity
of those who follow it to emerge.
If it were a path of interference and control,
those who tried to follow it would be miserable
and would soon turn aside.

What we call good fortune and bad fortune
are mixed together in all events.
If we try to have one without the other,
we will become completely confused
and everyone's suffering will increase.

The one who follows this path
will have firm principles,
but will never impose them
or injure others in their name;
will be honest, but never cruel;
will be consistent,
but never at the expense of others;
will be a guide to people,
but never overshadow them.

Moderation is the best way
to care for our affairs.
It frees us from fixed plans
that waste our power.
We never punish ourselves
for things we do or don't do,
so our power remains available.
With it we can respond
to the shifting winds of life
and use everything for good.

We are able to take care of our affairs,
no matter how complicated,
with the gentle ease
of a mother caring for her child.

Deeply rooted in our practice,
we never become confused
or lose our way.

We take care of our most important affairs
in the same way we fry a small fish.
We don't force the issue.
We don't hurry the process.

Our conditioned thoughts
of worry and of doubt
have lost their power.
We still notice them arising,
but they no longer run our lives.

Because we walk along this path,
that which used to make us suffer
has been transformed into wisdom.

61 ■ Everyone Is Welcome

A country centered in this path
is like a fertile valley.
All the world flows to it
and finds a place of rest and welcome.
Its stillness and tranquility
overcome the restlessness around it
and all find lasting peace.

This is our path of life.
We flourish not by pretending to be grand,
but by making a welcoming space for all.
When we bow a welcome to a stranger,
the stranger becomes a friend.
When the stranger bows a welcome in return,
we become a friend.
Everyone is welcome.
Everyone is home.

This path is the source of all that is.
It is the refuge of those who follow it.
It is the protector of those who ignore it.

We honor those
who show no interest in this path
with gentle words and loving-kindness.

Greater than any gift of wealth or power
is the quiet offering of ourselves to one another.
Two truths guide our practice:
"Look inside and you will find,"
and
"You are free of fault."

For this reason this path
is dear to us beyond all else.

Action on this path unfolds without effort.
Work is accomplished without strain.
Life is enjoyed without clinging.
The smallest things are honored
and the greatest things are seen as ordinary.
Ill treatment is seen
as an opportunity for kindness.
Small steps lead to great accomplishments.
Difficult tasks are seen
as a series of easy steps.
Therefore we pay complete attention
to the task in front of us.

There is no frivolous way to end our suffering.
By giving ourselves to the present moment,
this is exactly what we do,
for ourselves and for all beings.

Sitting still allows us to notice
the subtle stirrings of the mind.
Small thoughts that lead to suffering
are seen early and easily set aside.
Since trouble begins in the mind,
we watch the mind with care
and trouble is stopped before it begins.

This practice seems so passive and still.
Yet it is the seedling
from which the great tree grows.
It is the single small step
that begins the journey of a thousand miles.

If we hurry or force our practice,
it slips away from us.
We release ideas
of success and failure.
We patiently take the next necessary step
and everything unfolds as it should.
We lay down our wanting
and pick up our contentment.
We lay down our conditioning
and pick up our true nature.

We gently help all beings everywhere
return to their true nature.

The great teachers of this path
taught with humble simplicity.
No cathedrals, no books, no ado at all.
Just one person talking to another
about ordinary life.

Today the experts babble
about everything under the sun,
seeking to gather crowds
and control circumstances by their clever words.
Everyone is cheated.

We are truly blessed only
by one who teaches
from the heart.
This one reveals
the secrets of the universe:
how all forms and all beings
express the power of the Tao
by the fullness of their life,
and then return to their source.
The heart of our teaching
is to live in fullness
and return in joy.

Streams and rivers carve ravines and canyons
because they flow down to the ocean.
The power is in the downward flow.

One who helps us with this practice
speaks and acts with humility.
Therefore our own power flows.
One who leads us on this path
follows along behind.
Therefore our own true nature leads.

Our gratitude to the countless beings
who have transmitted this path
down to the present day
is without limit.
They taught with gentleness and grace.
Few of their names are known.
Great is their honor.

No one sees anything special about this path.
Yet it is because it appears ordinary
that it remains wondrous.
No one has been able to market it.
No one has trivialized it.

There are three virtues inherent in this path:
compassion, simplicity, and patience.
Wherever there is compassion,
fear does not abide.
Wherever there is simplicity,
generosity resides.
Wherever there is patience,
all things are accomplished.

If we try to be fearless
and do not have compassion,
we become ruthless.
If we try to be generous
and do not have simplicity,
we become controlling.
If we try to accomplish things
and do not have patience,
we become failures.

Compassion is the root of all these virtues.
It is the very nature of the Tao.
It is the energy that binds all things together.

When confrontation arises
we face it without aggression.
When someone opposes us
we do not give in to anger.
We view no one as a competitor
because we do not seek our own way.

We know our strengths
and we know our weaknesses.
We use them each for benefit.
We are not trying to fix ourselves or others
so we move naturally and easily along our path.

69 ▪ Call No One Enemy

Military strategists agree.
They would rather defend
than make a foolish attack.
They would rather consolidate
than overextend.

So we move forward
without conquering anyone.
We gain
without anyone losing.
We confront obstacles
without using weapons.

We call no one enemy,
for to call someone enemy
is to lose our inner unity.
We become divided against ourselves
and everyone suffers.

When conflict arises
we refuse to separate ourselves.
This is how we remain at peace.

Our conditioned ways
of seeing things and doing things
make it hard for us to understand.
But this path is easy to find
and easy to follow.

This path arises from the source of all.
Its power enlivens all things.
If we learn to know this source,
we learn to know ourselves.

Following this path we are led
to the inner treasure of our being.
Our outer trappings remain simple
so we are free to cherish our inner joy.

If we pretend to be aware
but do not recognize
our own suffering,
we remain ignorant.

The fundamental joy of this path is the awareness
of the suffering caused by our own mind.
Knowing its origin,
we know its ending.

If we have no awe of the mystery,
we are easily controlled by fear.
We constrict ourselves with self-hate
and become willing victims of other people.

Knowing our true nature,
we see ourselves clearly,
but do not become arrogant.
We cherish ourselves,
but not as separate from all other beings.
Our external identity
is nourished by our inner reality.

We do the best we can
yet sometimes our actions seem harmful.
At other times
they seem beneficial.
We find no answer as to why this is so.
We are only shown the way to walk
one step at a time,
accepting both harm and benefit
as essential parts of life.
We are shown how to remain quiet
yet respond to every situation.
We are shown how to be present
even before we are called.
We are shown how to be patient
yet accomplish everything.

The mysteries and unknowns
along this path are many,
yet on it we will never lose our way.

Our true nature does not fear death.
Our conditioned mind creates this fear
in a futile attempt to control events
and keep people in line.

Death is a natural part of this path.
An unnatural fear of death leads only to killing.
It is like trying to use the intricate tools
of a master craftsman.
We will surely cut ourselves.

Why do the poor lack what they need?
Because the rich consume too much.
Why do people become restless and discontent?
Because those in power try to control
every aspect of their lives.

Everyone is so concerned
with getting and keeping
that no one learns to really live before they die.

To follow this path
we must abandon overconsumption
and embrace true simplicity.

Before we are conditioned
by all the "dos and don'ts" of life,
we are naturally tender and gentle.
As we grow old,
we constrict around these conditions
and end up dying stiff and rigid.
Indeed all living things begin soft and supple
and end up brittle and dry.

So we see that hardness and inflexibility
are signs of death,
and that tenderness and gentleness
are signs of life.

It is the ability of an army to change its plans
that keeps it from defeat.
It is the ability of a tree to bend in the wind
that keeps it from toppling.
Our natural tenderness
is our true strength.

Following this path is like stringing a bow.
One end is pulled down
and the other is pulled up,
creating a dynamic balance.
So this practice encourages a dynamic balance
between excess and deficiency.
When we see an excess,
we reduce it.
When we see a deficiency,
we give to it.

This is contrary to common wisdom.
Common wisdom seeks
to constantly increase excess.
To do this, that which is lacking
must decrease even more.
Balance is destroyed.

To keep balance we must trust this path
and keep to our true nature.
This allows us to give without worry,
and to receive without attachment.

This path seems paradoxical.
Like water, it is soft and yielding,
yet there is no better way to overcome
the stiffness and rigidity
that causes so much suffering.

We intuitively know that flexibility
is more effective than stubbornness
and that tenderness is superior
to hard-heartedness,
yet our conditioned habits keep us
from acting on this knowledge.

By accepting all that seems humble and plain,
we become masters of every situation.
By opening our hearts
to all that seems painful and difficult,
we help end all suffering.
No wonder it seems paradoxical.

Resentment always leads
to more resentment.
Only contentment leads
to contentment.
Therefore we do not seek advantage or control.
Our contentment is independent
of the actions of others.
Seeking a special position
is not the way of life.

There are no "special favorites" along this path.
It unfolds itself before whoever walks along it.

The present moment is all we have,
so we are not constantly seeking
a faster way to do things
or a better place to be.
Our vehicles sit idle except when truly needed,
and our weapons remain locked away.

Our attention is always on
the experience of the moment
so we enjoy our food,
our clothing,
our homes,
and every aspect
of a simple way of living.

Though the world is filled
with sights we haven't seen,
we die content because
we have truly lived.

The most helpful words
do not please our conditioning.
Words that please our conditioning
are not helpful.
This path is not taught by argument.
Those who argue are not teaching this path.
Books cannot teach this path.
If we rely on books
we will not find this path.

Simplicity is our joyous and practical guide.
Therefore we always have enough
to live with generosity.
In this way our path brings great gain
yet does no harm.
No longer striving for control,
we discover life to be an ever-flowing river.

3 ▪ The Practice

My wife, Nancy, and I are in residence as teaching guides at the Still Point Center in Chico, California. If you lived nearby you would have the opportunity to sit in meditation with us twice each day. You could take part in one of our monthly workshops or attend an extended day of meditation. You could drop in to any of several weekly classes. You could do working meditation in our Zen Garden. You would be able to make an appointment for an individual session of exploration and guidance.

You might especially enjoy our ongoing study of the *Tao Te Ching*. Each week we look in detail at one chapter from Lao-tzu's book in a relaxed and informal setting. We sit with the text, in several translations, and talk about whatever arises in us. As a teaching guide, it is my responsibility to help each student clarify and understand the thoughts or feelings that arise. It is not my job to explain, to fix, to direct, or to supply the "correct" thought. I simply help.

The Still Point has been in existence for four years now and we are in our third read through Lao-tzu. Each time we reach the end of chapter 81, we start back again at chapter 1 and find the study an entirely new experience. I would project that ten years from now we will be on our eighth time through, still discovering and still awakening.

In this section you and I will explore Lao-tzu's work in much the same manner as we do in this weekly class. I have selected a sentence from each chapter and added a few brief comments and questions, much as I would in class. These comments and questions do not begin to exhaust the content of each chapter, but they do provide suggestions as to how you might approach the text.

We will explore the chapters in the order they appear in the text, just as we do in class. This will help us appreciate the nonlinear nature of this path. Themes will circle around and reappear when we least expect them. We will be aware that we are not on a simple "fix-it" approach to controlling our life. We are on a mysterious journey, one step at a time, never knowing exactly what the next step will be until we take the current one. But we will trust the path, the practice, and each other.

MEDITATION

In this section I also offer brief breath mantras for your meditative practice at the end of each chapter section. These mantras are helpful if recited silently in rhythm with your breath as you sit quietly in meditation. I recommend the most basic of meditation styles—simply sit or stand comfortably and let your attention keep returning to your breathing. Don't try to empty your mind or to resist your thoughts. Just notice when your thoughts carry you away into conditioned habits, stories, dramas, worries, plans, etc., and gently return to your breathing. Use a breath mantra if you find it helpful. Or simply think, "I'm breathing . . . I'm breathing . . . I'm breathing . . ."

An Intimate Conversation

I am attempting, notwithstanding the limitations of time, distance, and the printed word, to be present with you as we practice this path. As I write these words I imagine that we are in a comfortable and quiet place, much like our meditation hall. There is a simple flower display on a table beside us. I welcome you and honor you with a bow and we sit down to have a relaxed conversation. Please use your own imagination to join me. Sit comfortably and imagine we are in this quiet place together and that we have each other's full attention. Prepare yourself a cup of tea and imagine that we are sharing that as well. Use my brief suggestions to trigger your own internal dialogue. Raise a question. Listen for guidance. The true guide lives within you and you already have whatever guidance you need. Trust yourself. Take the next step.

CHAPTER ONE

**Talking about a path
is not walking that path.
Thinking about life
is not living.**

We don't practice to stop thinking and talking. We practice to turn our attention to the ways in which we have learned to think and talk. We watch how these conditioned habits distract us from actually living our life and substitute an obsession with ideas about our life.

■ Try asking this question over and over during the day: "Am I living right now, or am I thinking about living?" See if you can detect the subtle difference.

I have my thoughts . . . but I am not my thoughts.

Chapter Two

**Everything gives rise to its opposite,
therefore we work without conscious effort . . .**

Unconscious resistance to an action always accompanies that very action. It is difficult to take what might be called pure action that encompasses and accepts the opposites inherent in life. Accepting these opposites, we are able to do helpful things without second-guessing or thinking, "It shouldn't be this way." We stop trying to make things better and our actions end up improving life for everyone.

- What things in your experience seem ugly and without virtue? How do you respond to these things?
- Do you notice a degree of resistance, second-guessing, and effort as you seek to take helpful action?

Accepting everything . . . I accomplish everything.

CHAPTER THREE

**It frees us from our wanting
and returns us to our passion.**

To the degree that our thoughts are caught up in *wanting* something, or someone, we are unable to be fully present with the something or someone that is actually here, now. Conversely, to the degree that we are fully present in the moment, our wants disappear.

- Think of a time when you were completely absorbed in what you were doing. Bring that feeling back to your mind. Can you remember how and when that feeling disappeared, and how your thoughts turned away from the moment toward something else in the future?
- Turn your attention to your breathing and to the present moment. You are reading this book. Is there something else you want to be doing? Can you gently pull away from that wanting for the moment?

Releasing wanting . . . returning to passion.

Chapter Four

**Walking this path,
we experience inexhaustible energy.**

What Lao-tzu calls a "void" is actually a state of awareness where all of our conditioned ideas of who we are drop away. As we approach it, we often feel terrified, as if we will no longer exist, so we veer away through resistance and distraction. It is this use of energy to veer away that frustrates and exhausts us. If we are able to drop this resistance, we might be surprised at the energy that becomes available to us.

- There are undoubtedly parts of you that do not want a spiritual practice. They want to "make life work." Can you notice how they might cause you to veer away? Can you sense the fatigue involved?

Entering emptiness . . . finding fullness.

CHAPTER FIVE

**Therefore we welcome
everything and everyone
without distinction.**

Perhaps it would help to distinguish between "welcoming" and "enjoying." No one wants the difficult, unpleasant, and painful parts of life. But when, despite our efforts to prevent them they arise, well . . . here they are. No need to pretend to enjoy them, or to approve of them. Perhaps we could just be willing to accept them as part of "what is" at the moment, and therefore to lessen the psychic energy spent trying to constrict and squeeze them out.

- Notice the elements of your life that are "not welcome" at the moment. Sometimes this "not welcome" feeling is associated with a tightness and tension in the belly, chest, shoulders, or forehead. Without pushing away your feelings, can you soften this tension just a bit?

Welcoming everything . . . misery departs.

CHAPTER SIX

**There is no need
to weary ourselves in an effort to find her.
She is ever with us
because she *is* us.**

We often talk of a spiritual path as a search for the divine. There is nothing wrong with searching, but Lao-tzu would suggest that this process could keep us always one step behind, always identified with being a "seeker." He would not describe this practice as "seeking" anything. For him it is a practice of "finding." It is discovering that in each and every moment there is nothing to seek because everything is already here.

> ▪ What if seeking after the divine is actually a way of keeping yourself from the divine? What if the longings of your heart could be satisfied this very moment, in this very breath? Can you sense how that might feel?

Nothing to seek . . . everything is here.

CHAPTER SEVEN

Therefore, when they arise,
we watch.
When they pass away,
we remain.

This watching is not at all dispassionate. We are allowed to feel anything and everything. We are merely advised not to *identify* with anything that is transient, such as feelings, opinions, personalities, situations, etc. For instance, notice the subtle difference between "I'm feeling fear" and "I am afraid."

- Are there certain feelings or situations that, at the moment, you are identifying with rather than merely experiencing?

The Tao and I . . . remain.

CHAPTER EIGHT

**In this manner, our life flows like water
and fulfills itself naturally.**

Arranging our lives with a degree of simplicity and gentle kindness allows us to flow more naturally through the day. We still make choices and still take action. But we do it without undue struggle and without second thoughts. We don't have to find fulfillment. Fulfillment arises naturally from our experience of the moment—the "filled-full-moment."

- Are there ways that you are looking for fulfillment? What does that term mean for you?
- Can you touch that sense of "filled-full" living right now?

Life . . . is full.

CHAPTER NINE

**Working without thought of praise or blame
is the way of true contentment.**

Praise and blame are the cornerstones of identity formation. It is almost impossible to sense what life would be like if these poles were removed. Even as I write these words I hear a voice in my head that whispers, "Without praise and blame no one would know how they were supposed to live." Yet might it not be possible for us to mature in our behavior without the constant use of carrots and sticks? Is there something within us that naturally delights in helpful action?

- How does the process of looking for praise and avoiding blame restrict your life? Look especially at the ways you praise and blame yourself. (Remember, this is a gentle process. No blaming yourself for praising and blaming yourself!)

Letting go . . . being free.

Chapter Ten

**Can we embrace both the acceptable
and unacceptable parts of ourselves?**

It is important to note that this practice is not about changing ourselves. It is about opening ourselves to the wonder of life as it really is and to the wonder of who we really are. This is very difficult for most of us. We are products of millennia of conditioning that tells us that, if we don't struggle against our basic nature, we will suffer. Notice two assumptions that you might unconsciously be making. The first is that, if you accept yourself just as you are, you will not change. The second is that, if you accept yourself as you are, you will act in hurtful and harmful ways.

- What if these assumptions are not true?
- What "parts" of yourself are the most difficult to accept? Do you hear a voice that says, "You must not accept these parts. You must change them or they will destroy you?" What if that voice is wrong?

Trusting myself . . . I become myself.

CHAPTER ELEVEN

**We practice with the visible and tangible,
but it is the invisible and intangible within us
that bring us life.**

In order to catch a glimpse of the spiritual nature of existence, we observe ordinary things and events. For Lao-tzu, it is the *moving* of the wheel; the *emptying and filling* of the bowl; and the *living* in the home that are the essential qualities. The wheel, bowl, and home are merely tangible expressions of these intangible qualities. It is not an esoteric or mysterious practice. It is simply a matter of spending a few extra moments to look deeply at the ordinary.

- What are you doing right now? Where are you? Pretend I am on the phone with you. Tell me what you see as you look around.
- Now tell me about the intangibles. What qualities lie beneath the things you see?

Looking deeply . . . living fully.

CHAPTER TWELVE

**Attempting to satisfy all our appetites,
we become weary.**

So much of our cultural conditioning insists that satisfaction is
possible if we just try a little harder. Yet, no matter how hard we
try, there is always something else to do to satisfy the external or
internal voices. The only way out is to see the process for what
it is: a setup for dissatisfaction. What keeps us churning along
like hamsters on a wheel is the unconscious belief that
somehow, "This is going to work."

- If you're still trying to satisfy every internal and external
  voice it is because there is a part of you that still believes
  it will pay off. How is this belief reinforced?
- How might it be held more lightly?

I am the stillness . . . beneath the striving.

CHAPTER THIRTEEN

**Seeing ourselves as separate and isolated
makes us suffer.**

Might the feeling of separateness from the universe that makes us feel so vulnerable and anxious actually be a learned habit, a conditioned way of seeing? What if we were not skin-enclosed "things" to whom life is happening, but instead were part of life itself as it happens moment to moment?

- How might your experience of life be different if that were true?
- I am sitting by the window at a coffee shop in downtown Chico, California, writing these words. You are somewhere right now, reading these words. You are reading "now." I am writing "now." Are we really so separate?

I am part . . . of all I see.

CHAPTER FOURTEEN

**To realize our true nature,
we need only return to our breath,
here and now.**

Breathing is the most natural and effective gateway to the experience of the present moment. All of our esoteric speculations fall away when we turn to the simple experience of breathing in and breathing out. It is profoundly simple. But it is a simplicity that is terribly difficult to practice. Conditioned mental habits continually pull us into the realm of "looking for something."

- I am going to spend the next five minutes just sitting here breathing—not writing, not thinking about writing—just breathing. Join me.
- During the past five minutes, I watched my mind take me to at least a dozen different places—to magazine articles, movies, fears, and conversations with friends. Each time I drifted off I returned my attention to my breathing and just sat here. What was the five minutes like for you?

Breathing in . . . I am here.

**. . . we sit patiently and wait
for muddy thoughts to settle
and our mind to become clear.
Life then lives itself in us.**

Enlightenment, for Lao-tzu, is simply paying careful attention
to life. Simplicity and patience are essential. When all the conditioned noise, stress, pressure, and tension fade away, what is
left is freedom. But don't become trapped by impatiently
seeking patience or by making resolutions and rules about simplicity. There is nowhere you have to go and no one you have
to become. It all belongs to you already.

- What might it feel like to be free from worry and completely absorbed by each moment of living? Use your
  imagination and describe as completely as you can
  what your life would be like.
- Is there anything outside you that actually stands
  between you and this experience of life?

No thing to do . . . no one to be.

CHAPTER SIXTEEN

**Discovering our true nature,
we are at home
and nothing in life disturbs us.**

Our center here in Chico, California, is called the Still Point. Here we try to create an atmosphere where the qualities of quietness, openness, and compassion mentioned in this chapter have an opportunity to emerge. These qualities cannot be generated or forced. They are inherent in our true nature and only by returning to an awareness of this nature will we experience them.

- Let your hands rest over your abdomen just below your navel. Beneath your hands, about halfway through your body, is a "still point"—the center around which your body moves. There is also a still point about which your life moves. When do you feel it? How does it feel?

Home is . . . a place of stillness.

CHAPTER SEVENTEEN

**Hating our self,
how can we value anyone else?**

Are we really being helpful to the world when, absolutely unconscious of our own pain and self-hate, we become fervently involved in *helping others* and *making the world better?* We can give the world no greater gift than our own unconditional self-acceptance. As that occurs, our actions become unconditional as well. Free of strings, these actions allow others to accept themselves. Accepting themselves, they act from their true natures. The world is healed.

- Internal and external voices will suggest that a path of spiritual awareness is "self-indulgent." What effect do these voices have?
- What if these voices are merely authoritative-sounding distractions designed to keep you stuck?
- Is self-awareness the same thing as self-indulgence?

Aware of my self . . . I am aware of all.

CHAPTER EIGHTEEN

**When we forget who we truly are,
we turn to external rules . . .**

You may notice a tendency to look through this book for the rules and strategies. "Somewhere in here," you hope, "he will come clean and tell me what steps to take, how to take them, and where they will lead."

Sorry. In this practice there is only one rule: *We will use everything in our experience to reveal to us the ways we resist and avoid our life so that we might drop that resistance and avoidance and live with freedom and joy.*

■Is there anything going on in your life right now that might benefit from the application of this rule?

Everything I experience . . . brings me freedom.

Chapter nineteen

**We see through our conditioned mind
and find our true nature waiting.**

We are not trying to be holy. We are not trying to be good. We are not trying to be clever. We are not trying to be *anything!* We are practicing the process of returning, over and over, to the present moment. In this moment we are our true self and all the kindness necessary to heal the world is naturally ours.

- What qualities are you trying to cultivate in yourself?
- What would it feel like to stop trying to do that?

I am the one . . . who is waiting for me.

Chapter Twenty

**But this practice asks us to relinquish the illusion of control
and to be content with whatever comes our way.**

I wish I could promise holiness or financial reward as an incentive for walking this path. It offers only the reality behind the spiritual and material striving to which we are conditioned. It offers peace, rather than the things and situations we think will make us feel peaceful.

- Do you actually want peace and contentment? Or do you want the things and situations that you have come to believe will give you peace and contentment? Can you tell the difference?

Forsaking control . . . finding true peace.

CHAPTER TWENTY-ONE

**We know the truth of this way,
not by believing it,
but by being it.**

This journey into the heart of our true nature seems dark and foreboding only because it has been hidden for so long by the mental habits we have had for decades. We are going deeper into the heart of life than any belief has ever, or will ever, take us. We are becoming that which we seek.

- How might it feel to never again use the word "believe?"
- Can you imagine other words or phrases that you might substitute?

Losing belief . . . discovering trust.

Chapter Twenty-Two

**Acceptance of life
is the only path to wholeness.**

This practice redefines the word "perfection." It no longer means "the way I want it to be." It now means "the way it is." Our conditioning will tell us that this acceptance is actually resignation. Not true. Resignation is actually a very different process. Resignation leads to immobilization. Acceptance leads to action.

■ Practice with a situation in your life or in the world that is very difficult for you. Notice the difference in energy between saying out loud "I accept that this is the way it is right now" and saying "I am resigned to this."

Accepting what is . . . creating what is not yet.

CHAPTER TWENTY-THREE

**Success and failure are seen
as part of a seamless joyful whole.**

The words "success" and "failure" will lose their meaning as we continue our practice. Every experience can be a mirror in which we see how we separate ourselves from life. Every experience becomes an opportunity to drop our resistance, restriction, and separation.

- What things about your conditioning do you see when you "succeed?"
- What things about your conditioning do you see when you "fail?" (Remember it is the seeing, not the content, that sets us free.)

Using everything . . . setting myself free.

CHAPTER TWENTY-FOUR

**The very freedom it promises does not appear
until we lay it down.**

This practice does not indulge our need to get somewhere or
to be somebody. We must look carefully at the voices that are
urging us to become spiritual or to improve ourselves so we
are more acceptable. These voices pretend to speak for our
betterment, but they are in error. They are merely part of the
continual attempts to "do it right" we have learned to make
since childhood.

- Perhaps the most difficult task in this whole practice is
  the laying down of the idea of self-improvement. What
  things about yourself are you trying to improve?
- How might this keep you stuck?

Not gaining freedom . . . accepting it.

CHAPTER TWENTY-FIVE

**This path is our true home
because it is home to all things
in heaven and on earth.**

Our practice will never set us apart from any other being. We affirm that all living beings are being led, in their own way, along this path. This affirmation is contrary to the habit we all have of assuring ourselves we are going in the right direction by seeing how others are going in the "wrong" direction.

- Who do you set apart as "them"—wrong, ignorant, or deluded?
- How does this affect your experience of life?

There is no "them". . . only us.

Chapter Twenty-Six

**We have everything we could want.
Why would we scurry about
looking for something else?**

We are following a deep and venerable tradition, so we honor it with our full attention and devotion. At the same time we don't have to do this practice "right." We can drop our struggle and self-condemnation. When we become unconscious and captive to our conditioning (and we will . . . over and over), we merely notice it and return to our awareness. No problem.

- What voices right now are urging you to go somewhere else, do something else, pay attention to something else?
- Can you notice these voices without believing them?

All I need . . . I have within me.

CHAPTER TWENTY-SEVEN

**Ceasing to pick and choose:
this is the great secret of life.**

The annoying, or even dangerous, people and situations in our lives are not merely object lessons in correct and incorrect behavior. They are concrete representations of the fear, sadness, and suffering that arise from the conditioned idea that we are separate from life. They are here to teach us compassion, not moral lessons.

- Consider the situations and people that are difficult for you right now.
- What feelings of judgment do you notice?
- What feelings of compassion do you notice?

Seeing everything . . . with compassion.

CHAPTER TWENTY-EIGHT

**Separate from our true nature,
we create forms and functions
and struggle to make them work.**

Creating and crafting the things of life is not a problem. It can be a joy to design and fashion anything from a simple toy to a complex business. If we experience a sense of constant struggle in this process, however, it might be good to ask deeper questions.

- Is your work arising from your connection to and compassion for all beings, or is it emerging from an anxiety that insists you are separate and always at risk?

Doing . . . what is mine to do.

Chapter Twenty-Nine

**Our practice is to see all this
without taking it seriously.**

Not taking our ups and downs seriously does not mean that we see it all as trivial. Our joys and sorrows are very real and we must fully feel them all. However, we do not have to tell ourselves stories about these ups and downs as if we were the characters in a drama. In a drama we are able to stand outside the story and hope for a satisfying conclusion. In real life there is no static conclusion. One moment leads to the next, ever and always changing. Who knows if even death is a conclusion? Why box it in with stories? Why not just experience it?

- What stories are you telling yourself about the events of your life right now?
- How do these stories stop you from fully experiencing your life?

Fully present . . . fully alive.

CHAPTER THIRTY

To struggle is to invite resistance.
To invite resistance is to create suffering . . .

Some experiences are difficult. Some are extremely difficult. This is not a problem and does not create suffering. Struggle and suffering occur when some conscious or unconscious part of us resists the way we go about managing the difficulty.

For instance:

1. "This is what I intend to do."
2. "But I *can't* do that. It isn't fair!"

1. "There is nothing I can do right now."
2. "But there must be *something!*"

- What difficulties are you facing that you are turning into struggles?

Difficult . . . is not a problem.

CHAPTER THIRTY-ONE

**Once a battle is over we lay our weapons down
and weep that this has happened.**

Whenever we experience fear we look for someone or something outside ourselves to call "enemy." This enemy enables us to imagine some sense of control over our fear. We feel that if we can defeat the enemy, we can conquer the fear. Once we have created an enemy, violence is just around the corner.

- What might it be like to experience fear and not look for an enemy?
- What might it be like to be attacked by another person, to protect our selves, and still not have an enemy? How might that change the nature of our response?

No one . . . is my enemy.

CHAPTER THIRTY-TWO

**When we stop taking distinctions seriously,
we cease to suffer.**

To search for peace is to remain outside peace. It is like the classic story of the person riding on a bicycle looking high and low for a bicycle to ride. We *are* at peace. There is no other place to be that is real.

- Have you known people who have been at peace while dying?
- If that is possible, can there ever be a moment when choosing peace is not an option?

Nothing between . . . me and peace.

CHAPTER THIRTY-THREE

**Overcoming other people
requires force.
Overcoming our conditioning
requires true power.**

It is interesting to notice that our conditioning will quickly call a deepening self-awareness "self-indulgent." It then turns around and calls what is actually egocentric indulgence "realism." Seeing ourselves clearly is the only way to experience our personal power.

- As you continue to pursue a spiritual practice, what sort of internal criticisms do you notice?
- How do these criticisms keep you from experiencing your own power and capability?

I am capable . . . for my life.

CHAPTER THIRTY-FOUR

It is the true home to which we return,
yet it wants no worship.
No wonder we consider it great.

The desire to express gratitude is a natural human quality. Formal and informal rituals of worship help us in this expression as long as we remember that it is not about pleasing the Tao. It is about encouraging our selves to live with attention and mindfulness.

- What formal or informal rituals do you observe that keep you connected to beauty, silence, gratitude, and compassion? These are the worship services of this practice.

I worship in . . . each breath I take.

CHAPTER THIRTY-FIVE

**We turn to this path
only when we have exhausted
all other paths.**

A practice of awakening and awareness will never be popular and resistance to such a practice is normal. We will struggle for contentment and fight for peace as long as we continue to believe that contentment and peace are the result of finally getting control of life.

- Do you sense the resistance to this practice within yourself?
- What does this resistance say about what you should be doing instead?
- How does it keep you stuck?

Nothing exciting . . . merely peace.

Chapter Thirty-Six

**If we try to get rid of something,
it will naturally remain.**

Our conditioning insists that, unless we use willpower to push away and resist thoughts and habits we label harmful, we will: become a drunk, go blind, end up on the street, land in jail, be worthless, get fat, etc. This practice suggests that self-acceptance will succeed where willpower fails.

- Pick a habit you have tried to break for years without success. Spend the next month indulging in this habit whenever you want, *but refrain completely from any moralizing, scolding, or any other form of self-punishment.* Merely watch what happens. If, after a month, you are actually worse off, you can return to self-punishment. We all know how to do that.

Acceptance succeeds . . . resistance fails.

Chapter Thirty-Seven

**When our conditioning arises
and attempts to stir us up,
we return to the simple stillness
of our natural state.**

When we were children, we played all day and slept all night without conscious effort. That effortlessness remains available to us today.

- Recall a time when, as an adult, you were lost in some activity and unaware of the passage of time or of becoming tired.
- What stops you from experiencing more of life from that perspective? (There's nothing wrong here. We're not trying to fix something. We're just looking at the multitudes of ways in which we keep ourselves fatigued and distracted.)

Abundant energy . . . is always mine.

CHAPTER THIRTY-EIGHT

**Not trying to be good,
we experience natural goodness.**

"Try to be good" is the universal parent/teacher admonition to every boy and girl in our society. And every parent, teacher, and other authority figure has a different idea of just what "good" means. What if we didn't have to try to be good? What if our nature were goodness?

- What rules have you learned about being good?
- When and from whom did you learn these rules?
- What happens if you follow these rules?
- What happens if you don't follow these rules?
- What would you naturally do if you didn't have these rules?

My nature . . . is goodness.

CHAPTER THIRTY-NINE

**. . . we just roll along
like common stones in the river.**

Our conditioning fears that, if we are not noticed, we will cease to matter. So we use all of our energy to bring favorable attention to ourselves. This never achieves the desired results, and leaves us exhausted. What if we turned all that energy to the practice of awakening to our true nature?

- When and where in your daily experience do you sense the need to be noticed?
- When and where do you notice exhaustion beginning to set in?
- Becoming aware of these times allows you to practice bringing the energy of compassion and acceptance to yourself.

Within the Tao . . . I always belong.

Chapter Forty

**Everything in the cosmos
depends on everything else.**

Above all else in this practice, be tender and gentle with your-self. Have compassion for all the frightened and confused parts of yourself. There is no need to fix them or to get them to behave. Each is part of you, as you are part of everything that is.

- When I say, "Be tender and gentle with yourself," what exceptions do you find yourself wanting to make?
- How might the parts of life that you are pushing away be the most important for you?

All that is . . . is part of me.

Chapter Forty-One

**The most helpful response to this path
is to devote ourselves to it . . .**

Our conditioned mind will continually attempt to turn our attention to confusion, failures, obstacles, shame, inadequacies, suspicions, and uncertainty. I sometimes call this my "something wrong" mind. The paradoxical sayings in this chapter are helpful in seeing through this kind of conditioning.

■ Find an illustration from your life that shows the truth of each of the paradoxical sayings in this chapter.

The formless . . . brings me form.

Chapter Forty-Two

There is no gain without loss.
There is no fullness without deprivation.

We are assured by our culture that the successful life is the one that maximizes gain and minimizes loss. This practice assures us that gain and loss are built into the very fabric of existence. Wisdom lies in knowing how to let them come and go, rise and fall.

■ The most powerful example of the necessity of yin and yang each taking their place is the simple act of breathing. Think how absurd it would be to breathe for the next five minutes by inhaling only.

■ What other examples of the necessity of gain and loss

do you see in your life? What do you tell yourself about
these things?

Everything comes . . . everything goes.

Chapter Forty-Three

We act without ado.
We teach without arguments.

A question often arises for me: "Why write a book unless you are
arguing a point of view?" Yet when I put words on paper, the ones
that ring true for me are those that have no argumentative strings
attached. I can tell when I have slipped into needing to convince
you of something. We become separate, one standing here, one
standing there. Both of us suffer. Forgive me when that happens.

- What argumentative processes do you notice in your life?
- What does your conditioned mind tell you to get you to
  argue?
- How do you notice the difference between feeling or
  speaking passionately about a subject and needing to
  convince someone of something?

Speak with passion . . . and let it go.

CHAPTER FORTY-FOUR

Does wealth compensate
for the loss of ourselves?

There is nothing wrong with producing, selling, and buying products. The process we want to watch is the unconscious agreement we make with our conditioning that such activities will (1) mean something about who we are, and (2) lead to satisfaction.

- What do you tell yourself about your economic situation —how you earn a living and what you buy?
- Where did you learn these self-definitions?
- Are they true?

I am not . . . what I buy and sell.

CHAPTER FORTY-FIVE

**When we see clearly,
we act with tranquility,
and exactly what is needed is done.**

Our conditioned mind will tell us that we don't have the time
or energy to do all that "needs doing." This is not true. When
we see through our energy-sapping distractions we have all the
time and ability we need to do what is before us in the moment.

- Pay attention to the way in which first one task, and
  then another, and then another, get flashed on the
  screen of your mind, each clamoring for attention.
- What payoffs, negative and positive, do you get from
  this process?

I have all . . . the time I need.

Chapter Forty-Six

**To be content with each breath
is to be eternally content.**

The sentiment of this chapter is heresy to contemporary culture. Continuous discontent drives the economic engine, and we all cooperate in the process. Wanting more in the pursuit of contentment is the great tragedy of our time.

- My dear teacher, Cheri Huber, often tells me, "If you want contentment, be content. If you want more, get more. Just don't believe one process leads to the other." What do you believe you still need in order to be content?
- Some would say that contentment is not a good thing, that it stops progress. How do you see that belief working in you?

All of life . . . is in this breath.

Chapter Forty-Seven

**The more we look outside ourselves for knowledge,
the less we know about anything.**

If exploring new places and finding new information pleases us, we are certainly free to enjoy it. The problem arises when we think we are going to find something that we don't already have. There is nowhere we have to go but here and no one we have to find but our self.

- What makes you decide to travel, even on a short trip?
- What makes travel satisfying or dissatisfying for you?
- Does that same process of satisfaction/dissatisfaction operate in other areas of your life?

All I need . . . is in this moment.

CHAPTER FORTY-EIGHT

**Seeking the Tao,
we drop assumptions each day.**

Some of the common assumptions that we often don't question:

1. That we really know someone.
2. That we really know ourselves.
3. That someone else is right.
4. That someone else is wrong.

What assumptions do you make about:

1. How the day will unfold?
2. What you can and cannot do?
3. What another person will do?

Assuming nothing . . . gaining everything.

CHAPTER FORTY-NINE

**We extend trust to the trustworthy
and untrustworthy alike.
Thus trust becomes our very nature.**

Trusting another person to behave as we think they should behave will surely disappoint us. Trusting that another person's true nature, even when it is hard to see, is the same as ours will bring us joy and peace.

- How do people disappoint you?
- What do you do when you are disappointed in another person?
- What options might you have?

Trusting . . . opens possibilities.

CHAPTER FIFTY

Life and death are inseparable.
One is form and the other is formless.
Each gives way to the other.

Once an attacking soldier threatened a Taoist sage, brandishing his sword and yelling, "Don't you know you are facing one who can cut off your head without blinking an eye?" The sage smiled and said, "Don't you know you are facing one who can have his head cut off without blinking an eye?"

The soldier bowed before the sage.

- What assumptions do you make about death that constrict your life?
- What would your life be like if those assumptions were dropped?
- Might these assumptions be wrong?

Life and death . . . become the same.

Chapter Fifty-One

The Tao expresses itself
in each and every being.

We do not have to worry about pleasing or displeasing the Tao. Even when we are deeply caught up in our conditioned thoughts and behaviors, we remain expressions of the Tao. This enables authentic forgiveness and bestows marvelous freedom upon our lives.

- What memories do you keep of actions that remain shameful and unacceptable to you?
- What would your life be like if you knew that even these could not keep you from being a beloved expression of the Tao?

The Tao expresses . . . itself as me.

Chapter Fifty-Two

**If we follow our thoughts
and chase after distractions,
we will live in chaos.**

We have come to believe that our thoughts and memories are the essence of our identity. Consider the possibility that they may be guests who are merely passing through, not permanent squatters. Positive or negative, helpful or unhelpful, acceptable or unacceptable—they are all impermanent. When they leave, we remain.

- To which thought patterns and habits do you cling?
- How does this affect your life?

Thoughts pass through . . . I remain.

CHAPTER FIFTY-THREE

**It takes just a tiny bit of willingness
to follow this path,
but many things distract us.**

The fact that you and I are united by these words at this
moment in time means that we each have the willingness to
encounter this practice. You will go on to your distractions and
I to mine. But this little bit of willingness is all we need to keep
us returning to this path. And when we return, it will be as if we
had never left.

- Without punishing yourself, notice the ways in which
  you distract yourself from your practice.
- Notice also the ways in which you are willing to return.

Each distraction . . . is a chance to return.

CHAPTER FIFTY FOUR

**We see ourselves in every person we meet.
The whole world becomes our family,
our community,
our country.**

A practice of internal self-discovery is by its very nature a practice of connection to the whole world. Far from isolating us in a withdrawal from life, it connects us with the essence of life in all of its forms. All beings begin to seem as dear to us as our closest friends.

- Notice the people you meet today. What qualities, positive and negative, do you assume about each one?
- How are these qualities present in you? (No judgment here—just an increasing compassion for all, yourself included.)

I see myself . . . in all I meet.

CHAPTER FIFTY-FIVE

**Forcing events to be other than they are
only brings us misery.**

Harmony is not something we create. It can be seen in every moment if we are able to look deep enough. Even the desire to make some external change can arise from the essential harmony of our nature. As we act for change, it is important to look for the preexisting harmony.

- What seems out of harmony in your life?
- What changes do you want to make?
- Can you sense the essential harmony before you begin to make changes so that the changes are born in harmony rather than disharmony?

From what is . . . I make what is not.

Chapter Fifty-Six

**The more we understand this path,
the less we need to convince others.**

A good guideline for the depth of a practice in our life is noticing whether or not we are trying to convert others to our point of view. The need to convert is rooted in uncertainty and self-doubt. Enthusiasm is a natural feeling, but can slip into anxiety when others are seen to have their own, different views.

- What is the difference in your experience between honestly expressing your views and seeking to convince someone?
- What internal feelings and bodily senses accompany each?

I am me . . . you are you.

CHAPTER FIFTY-SEVEN

**. . . we stop trying to change ourselves
and find that we naturally change.**

A central paradox of our practice is that, by giving up any need to change or improve our lives, we find that change and improvement naturally occur. There is a natural process of goodness, peace, and abundance that is constantly at work within us. Our practice is to stop forcing this process.

- What would your life feel like if you were able to make all the fixes and improvements you desire?
- Can you let yourself feel that way now?

Nothing to change . . . everything changes.

CHAPTER FIFTY-EIGHT

**The one who follows this path
will have firm principles,
but will never impose them
or injure others in their name . . .**

Politicians piously intone "values" in an attempt to further a political agenda. In this practice we are urged to place all culturally conditioned values in a secondary role. We are free to have opinions and to share them appropriately, but never to impose them on others or judge others for not sharing them.

- What five personal qualities do you most value?
- What occurs in your life when others do not share these values?
- How might you live your life according to your values in a way that does not cause harm to yourself or others?

Do no harm . . . in the guise of values.

CHAPTER FIFTY-NINE

**We never punish ourselves
for things we do or don't do,
so our power remains available.**

Most of us have a deeply conditioned belief that, without self-punishment, there would be no self-improvement. It is the "beatings will continue until morale improves" school of life management, and it brings only suffering. Punishment never works. It gives only the illusion of control.

- Make a mental note of every time you tell yourself that you are doing, or about to do, something "wrong." Especially notice the subtle ones, like "I should have eaten there instead of here," or "I should have worn this instead of that."
- What would your life experience be like if all of these self-punishments were dropped?
- Would you become out of control, or would you just stop suffering?

Never a need . . . for punishment.

**. . . that which used to make us suffer
has been transformed into wisdom.**

A wise woman once told me, "Wisdom does not come from understanding everything, it comes from accepting everything." When confronted with this truth, we see that we often really don't want to become wise. We want to appear wise, while still trying to make life be what we want it to be.

- What if all the things that make you frustrated and unhappy were to remain in your life, but were no longer seen as problems?
- As an experiment, pick a particular issue and spend a day pretending, just pretending, that it is not a problem.

Problems . . . are not a problem.

Chapter Sixty-One

**We flourish not by pretending to be grand,
but by making a welcoming space for all.**

The need to appear grand and extraordinary is rooted in fear
and self-protectiveness. We come to believe that separating ourselves from others through our achievements and acquisitions
will keep us safe. We welcome into our lives only those people
and events that support our ideas and interests. This keeps us
separate from the actual experience that life presents us.

- What people and events are welcome in your life?
- What people and events are not welcome?
- How does this process affect your experience of life?

I have space . . . for all of life.

Chapter Sixty-Two

**It is the refuge of those who follow it.
It is the protector of those who ignore it.**

There is never a need to say to another person, "Walk this path."
All beings are unconsciously walking this path at every

moment. All are protected, guided, and nurtured in the same manner. This is why we can greet every person with esteem and honor.

- If all are walking this path already, why adopt this practice?
- In what ways might you find a "refuge" in this practice?

Here . . . I find refuge.

CHAPTER SIXTY-THREE

There is no frivolous way to end our suffering.
By giving ourselves to the present moment,
this is exactly what we do,
for ourselves and for all beings.

Awareness practice is the only way to actually connect with the world at large. A healing connection with other people must occur in the reality of the moment rather than in the conditioned ideas and projections of our minds. As we gently bring awareness to our own ways of restricting our lives, we release the power of our compassion into a waiting world.

- Do you notice internal voices that suggest that "you are selfish and should be doing more for others?"

- Have there been times when you have helped other people with a sense of freedom and energy? What was allowing that to happen?

There is no self . . . and other.

Chapter Sixty-Four

**If we hurry or force our practice,
it slips away from us.**

This practice is not one more thing we have to do well. It is not another ingredient in a successful and happy life. It is not the construction of a new and more pleasing set of beliefs. It is simply the conscious willingness to accept and fully live each moment of life.

- What is the single small step awaiting you at this moment? (For me it is the writing of the next few sentences of this exercise, nothing more.)
- What do the voices that take you away from the present moment imply? What techniques do they use?

The next small step . . . is all I do.

CHAPTER SIXTY-FIVE

**The heart of our teaching
is to live in fullness
and return in joy.**

No one will ever build great temples to honor this path. No one will build intricate organizational structures of priests and teachers. The temples already exist in the mountains, trees, rivers, and oceans of our world. The intricacy of the human body and the organizational structure of the cosmos are more than sufficient.

- What does your conditioned mind look for in a teacher—in a practice?
- What does your soul look for in a teacher—in a practice?

I live in fullness . . . and return in joy.

CHAPTER SIXTY-SIX

**One who leads us on this path
follows along behind.
Therefore our own true nature leads.**

If you see virtue in a teacher, it is because that virtue is already within you. If you sense power in another person, it is because you already know that power in your own being.

- List the qualities you admire in those you consider wise.
- Read each quality out loud, inserting before each, "I am . . ."
- Do you notice resistance to this exercise? What might be the origin of that resistance?

I am . . . that which I seek.

Chapter Sixty-Seven

Compassion is the root of all these virtues.
It is the very nature of the Tao.

Compassion is not sentimental, nor is it interested in our conditioned desires and wants. It is the energy that connects us with all of life. It enables us to live with open rather than restricted hearts. It gives us the ability to accept, to act, and to live with passion.

- When might compassion not appear "nice" according to our conditioned definitions?
- What differences do you notice between the conditioned idea of "virtue" and the real thing?

At the heart of all . . . compassion rests.

CHAPTER SIXTY-EIGHT

**When confrontation arises
we face it without aggression.**

It is easy to be peaceful and nonaggressive when people behave as we feel they should. The real opportunity to practice occurs when we encounter people who truly oppose or even attack us. Can we find a response that is nonaggressive yet still strong and centered?

- What might a nonaggressive response to confrontation look like?
- How would you avoid capitulation or injury while still not giving in to anger?

Without anger . . . I stand firm.

Chapter Sixty-Nine

**When conflict arises
we refuse to separate ourselves.**

When we classify people as enemies, we remove the pathways of understanding between us. We begin to judge their motives and actions through the filters of our own fears. Self-justification and self-protection become more important than openness and awareness.

- Consider those whose opinions, actions, motives, and lifestyles you deeply question—how might you remain connected with these people while honoring your own convictions?

In opposition . . . yet connected.

CHAPTER SEVENTY

**. . . this path is easy to find
and easy to follow.**

If we become identified with a conditioned ego identity that is invested in having life unfold in a certain way, we will struggle. We will even use this practice to try to "make" life go that way. When we return to simply breathing, noticing, and accepting, the struggle fades. This practice is difficult for our ego, easy for our true nature.

- What areas of your practice seem to be a struggle for you?
- What are you holding on to in these areas?

Easy to find . . . easy to follow.

CHAPTER SEVENTY ONE

**If we pretend to be aware
but do not recognize
our own suffering,
we remain ignorant.**

When we get caught up in our resistance to life we may think, "Here I am again! Will I never learn?" But each time we see the ways we resist and suffer, we are blessed. We have taken one more step toward clarity and freedom. We have one more wonderful opportunity to set aside our conditioned mental habits and glimpse, even if for only a moment, the freedom waiting for us.

- What opportunities to set aside your resistance and suffering lie before you right now?

Oh happy blessed . . . opportunity.

CHAPTER SEVENTY-TWO

**Our external identity
is nourished by our inner reality.**

The parts of us that respond with judgment and criticism do not need another layer of judgment piled upon them—"Stop being so judgmental and critical!" Our true nature is capable of unconditionally accepting our fearful responses while allowing kinder and more effective responses to emerge.

- Which of your responses over the past few days indicate parts of you that need acceptance?
- How might you accept these parts without letting them be in charge?

I nurture and accept . . . every part of me.

CHAPTER SEVENTY-THREE

**We are only shown the way to walk
one step at a time,
accepting both harm and benefit
as essential parts of life.**

Sometimes our best intentions actually cause harm, while our mistakes can unexpectedly bring benefit. There is no need to hold on to the idea that, if we can just avoid making mistakes, we can control life. This frees us to take the step we see before us without needing to know the unknowable future.

- What are you telling yourself about your mistakes and successes?
- How do you know this is true?

No need to grab . . . the future.

Chapter Seventy-Four

Death is a natural part of this path.

Our practice neither focuses on nor avoids death. Because we are learning to see clearly what is before us in the present moment, we let death take its place in the natural order of things. Birth and death are occurring at every moment, and we see that one always gives way to the other. We do what is before us. When it is time to die, we die with the same attention and wonder with which we have learned to do everything else.

- When you consider death, what conditioned fears ask for attention?
- Where and when did you learn these fears?
- How do they affect your experience of life?

I live and die . . . with complete attention.

CHAPTER SEVENTY-FIVE

**Everyone is so concerned
with getting and keeping
that no one learns to really live before they die.**

Lao-tzu would not judge our consumer culture as wrong. He would merely ask, "Where is this taking you?" He advises a truly simple life, not out of moralistic righteousness, but out of pragmatic compassion. Overconsumption arises from the need to assuage fear. Perhaps there are more effective ways to turn from fear to trust.

- In what ways do your fears complicate your life?
- What small steps might you take to simplify an area of your life? (Be prepared to look compassionately at the fears that arise to distract you.)

It is a gift . . . to be simple.

CHAPTER SEVENTY SIX

**Our natural tenderness
is our true strength.**

Aging is an interesting part of our practice. Some people seem to grow softer, gentler, and more accepting as they age, while others seem to become more fearful, opinionated, and isolated. Even though the body begins to slow down and present more difficulty, flexibility of mind and spirit can continue to increase.

- What path are you taking as you age?
- What are you doing to increase your mental and physical flexibility?
- How are you opening your mind and your heart?
- How are you involving yourself in your community?

Tenderness . . . is my strength.

CHAPTER SEVENTY-SEVEN

**When we see an excess,
we reduce it.
When we see a deficiency,
we give to it.**

Our lives work best when resources flow in and out at about the same rate. This does not mean that we spend recklessly or that we do not save for certain things. It means that we allow ourselves to give and receive without fear. It is our fearful conditioning that keeps us spending what we do not have and hoarding what we should be giving away.

- Where in your life do you have excess? (Money, time, skill, energy.) What might you do with it?
- Where do you have deficiency? How might you be open to receiving?

I give and receive . . . with equal ease.

CHAPTER SEVENTY-EIGHT

**By opening our hearts
to all that seems painful and difficult,
we help end all suffering.**

We do not assume that pain and difficulty are either bad or wrong. Therefore we do not have to find someone to blame for causing them or for not fixing them. Our energy is available for truly helpful action.

- Consider your own or a friend's difficulties. Who are you blaming or holding responsible?
- What if you dropped that, no matter how justified it seems? What might you be free to do?

Not blaming . . . I act with power.

Chapter Seventy-Nine

**Our contentment is independent
of the actions of others.**

We often spend many years seeking to create lives of contentment. We choose our friends, lovers, possessions, careers, politics, and beliefs with this in mind. It does not work. Now we turn to this practice and find that contentment is our true nature.

- To whom and to what are you looking for contentment?
- Changing nothing in your schedule, how would you
live today if you actually were content?

Contentment . . . is always possible.

CHAPTER EIGHTY

**Though the world is filled
with sights we haven't seen,
we die content because
we have truly lived.**

Going to new places and seeing new things can be wonderful.
The problem lies in going everywhere but seeing nothing.

- Pretend today that you are living in a completely new
  place and working at completely new tasks. See everything and everyone for the first time.
- Look constantly for that which you have never seen
  before, even if it is only a blue bicycle leaning against
  the white trunk of a sycamore.
- Notice the resistance that arises when you consider this
  experiment.

Everything is always . . . new and different.

CHAPTER EIGHTY-ONE

**The most helpful words
do not please our conditioning.
Words that please our conditioning
are not helpful.**

There is, of course, a place for beautiful and pleasing words. The question is: "Who is being pleased?" Words that support our opinions, beliefs, and judgments, no matter how enter- taining, contribute to our sense of separateness and thus are not truly helpful. Words that point us to our wholeness and unity are beautiful to our souls, but may be avoided, judged, and rejected by our conditioned minds.

- What words do you feed yourself daily?
- Who is being fed—the separate, fearful, judging self, or the compassionate all-embracing one?

Beautiful words . . . of life.

Afterword

Take the Next Step

There is a small step waiting for you right at this moment. It may be just closing this book and fixing yourself some lunch, or it may be returning to one of the chapters to explore an idea more fully. It may be going off to meet someone or settling in by yourself to meditate and reflect.

Whatever you do next will probably seem quite ordinary. There is no need for it to be otherwise. The wonder and extra-ordinariness will come from the attention and awareness you bring to it. Don't worry about transforming or changing your life. That will take care of itself. Don't get caught up in trying to fix yourself or anyone else. Neither you nor anyone else needs fixing. All the necessary change will unfold of its own accord if you can simply be present in your life.

May this book be a guide for you, but never substitute for your own wisdom. You are completely capable of anything your life brings you. You will never be truly lost and you will return to your true self without fail. May your journey be free of the suffering of resistance and control. May you find love and compassion waiting within you always.

Go ahead and take the next step.

About the Author

WILLIAM MARTIN has been a student of the Tao for almost twenty years. A graduate of the University of California, Berkeley, and of Western Theological Seminary, he is the author of, most recently, *The Parent's Tao Te Ching*, *The Couple's Tao Te Ching*, and *The Sage's Tao Te Ching*. Today he operates, with his wife, Nancy, the Still Point, a center for the practice of Taoist/Zen meditation in Chico, California.